Lecture Notes in Computer Science   9305

Commenced Publication in 1973
Founding and Former Series Editors:
Gerhard Goos, Juris Hartmanis, and Jan van Leeuwen

More information about this series at http://www.springer.com/series/7411

Magnus Jonsson · Alexey Vinel
Boris Bellalta · Olav Tirkkonen (Eds.)

Multiple Access Communications

8th International Workshop, MACOM 2015
Helsinki, Finland, September 3–4, 2015
Proceedings

 Springer

Editors

Magnus Jonsson
Halmstad University
Halmstad
Sweden

Alexey Vinel
Halmstad University
Halmstad
Sweden

Boris Bellalta
Universitat Pompeu Fabra
Barcelona
Spain

Olav Tirkkonen
Aalto University
Espoo
Finland

ISSN 0302-9743   ISSN 1611-3349   (electronic)
Lecture Notes in Computer Science
ISBN 978-3-319-23439-7   ISBN 978-3-319-23440-3   (eBook)
DOI 10.1007/978-3-319-23440-3

Library of Congress Control Number: 2015947116

LNCS Sublibrary: SL5 – Computer Communication Networks and Telecommunications

Springer Cham Heidelberg New York Dordrecht London

Printed on acid-free paper

Springer International Publishing AG Switzerland is part of Springer Science+Business Media
(www.springer.com)

Preface

It is our great pleasure to present the proceedings of the 8th International Workshop on Multiple Access Communications (MACOM), which was held in Helsinki during September 3–4, 2015. Previous events were organized in Halmstad (2014), Vilnius (2013), Maynooth (2012), Trento (2011), Barcelona (2010), Dresden (2009), and Saint-Petersburg (2008).

Our gratitude goes to the Technical Program Committee and external reviewers for their efforts in selecting 12 high-quality contributions (out of 18 submitted) to be presented and discussed at the workshop.

The contributions gathered in these proceedings describe the latest advancements in the field of multiple access communications, with an emphasis on wireless sensor networks, physical layer techniques, resources handling and allocation, medium access control protocols, and video coding.

Finally, we would like to take this opportunity to express our gratitude to all the participants, together with the local organizers, who helped to make MACOM 2015 a very successful event.

September 2015

Olav Tirkkonen
Alexey Vinel
Magnus Jonsson
Boris Bellalta

Organization

MACOM 2015 was organized by Aalto University, Finland.

Executive Committee

General Co-chairs

Olav Tirkkonen   Aalto, Finland
Alexey Vinel   HH, Sweden

TPC Co-chairs

Boris Bellalta   UPF, Spain
Magnus Jonsson   HH, Sweden

Local Chair

Ragnar Freij   Aalto, Finland

Publication Chair

Nikita Lyamin   HH, Sweden

Technical Program Committee

Konstantin Avrachenkov   INRIA Sophia Antipolis, France
Florin Avram   Université de Pau, France
Abdelmalik Bachir   Imperial College London, UK
Sandjai Bhulai   VU University Amsterdam, Netherlands
Giuseppe Bianchi   University of Rome "Tor Vergata", Italy
Torsten Braun   University of Bern, Switzerland
Raffaele Bruno   IIT-CNR, France
Peter Buchholz   TU Dortmund, Germany
Claudia Campolo   Università Mediterranea di Reggio Calabria, Italy
Cristina Cano   Hamilton Institute, Ireland
Periklis Chatzimisios   Alexander TEI of Thessaloniki, Greece
Young-June Choi   Ajou University, South Korea
Tugrul Dayar   Bilkent University, Turkey
Desislava Dimitrova   University of Bern, Switzerland
Alexander Dudin   Belarusian State University, Belarus
Marc Emmelmann   Fraunhofer FOKUS, Germany
Lorenzo Favalli   University of Pavia, Italy
Dieter Fiems   Ghent University, Belgium
Andres Garcia-Saavedra   Trinity College Dublin, Ireland
Marco Gramaglia   National Research Council of Italy, Italy

Geert Heijenk	University of Twente, Netherlands
Andras Horvath	University of Turin, Dip. di Informatica, Italy
Ganguk Hwang	KAIST, South Korea
Dragi Kimovski	University for Information Science and Technology - R. Macedonia, Macedonia
Valentina Klimenok	Belarusian State University, Belarus
Jarkko Kneckt	Nokia Research Center, Finland
Kristina Kunert	Halmstad University, Sweden
Douglas Leith	Hamilton Institute, Ireland
Arturas Medeisis	International Telecommunication Union, Saudi Arabia
Dmitry Osipov	IITP RAS, Russia
Evgeny Osipov	LTU Luleå University of Technology, Sweden
Edison Pignaton de Freitas	Federal University of Santa Maria, Brazil
Vicent Pla	Universitat Politecnica de Valencia, Spain
Zsolt Saffer	Budapest University of Technology and Economics, Hungary
Nikos Sagias	University of Peloponnese, Greece
Pablo Salvador	IMDEA Networks Institute, Spain
Bruno Sericola	INRIA Rennes - Bretagne Atlantique, France
Susanna Spinsante	Università Politecnica delle Marche, Italy
Andrey Trofimov	Saint-Petersburg State University of Aerospace Instrumentation, Russia
Bernhard Walke	RWTH Aachen University, Germany
Till Wollenberg	University of Rostock, Germany
Yan Zhang	Simula Research Laboratory and University of Oslo, Norway

Contents

MAC II

MAC I

Multi-objective and Financial Portfolio Optimization of Carrier-Sense Multiple Access Protocols with Cooperative Diversity

Ramiro Samano-Robles[1]([⊠]) and Atilio Gameiro[2]

[1] Research Centre in Real-Time and Embedded Computing Systems, Porto, Portugal
rasro@isep.ipp.pt
[2] Instituto de Telecomunicações, Campus Universitário, 3810-193 Aveiro, Portugal
amg@ua.pt

Abstract. This paper addresses a trade-off design and optimization of a class of wireless carrier-sense multiple access (CSMA) protocols where collision-free transmissions are assisted by the cooperative retransmissions of inactive terminals with a correct copy of the original transmission(s). Terminals are thus enabled with a decode-and-forward (DF) relaying protocol. The analysis is focused on asymmetrical settings, where terminals explicitly experience different channel and queuing statistics. This work is based on multi-objective and financial portfolio optimization tools. Each packet transmission is thus considered not only as a network resource, but also as a financial asset with different values of return and risk (or variance of the return). The objective of this financial optimization is to find the transmission policy that simultaneously maximizes return and minimizes risk in the network. The work presented here is focused on the characterization of the boundaries (envelope) of different types of trade-off performance region: the conventional throughput region, sum-throughput vs. fairness, sum-throughput vs. power consumption, and return vs. risk regions. Fairness is evaluated by means of the Gini-index, which is commonly used in economics to measure income inequality. Transmit power consumption is directly linked to the global transmission rate. The protocol is shown to outperform non-cooperative solutions under different network conditions that are discussed in detail in the main body of the paper.

Keywords: Cooperative diversity · Random access · Throughput region · Multi-objective and financial portfolio optimization

1 Introduction

1.1 Background and Open Issues

Wireless networks are rapidly evolving. Behind this quick evolution, there is a set of powerful, increasingly complex and adaptive physical (PHY) layer technologies. The study of advanced signal processing tools with multiple antennas,

© Springer International Publishing Switzerland 2015
M. Jonsson et al. (Eds.): MACOM 2015, LNCS 9305, pp. 3–18, 2015.
DOI: 10.1007/978-3-319-23440-3_1

cooperative users and interference control requires new cross-layer and cross-system design methodologies [1]. This means that the optimization of MAC and RRM algorithms should consider more details of the underlying PHY-layer. In addition, application layers are becoming increasingly heterogeneous, with different quality of service requests and different pricing policies. The number of metrics, parameters and issues to be simultaneously addressed is thus considerably large in comparison with legacy networks [2]. This already large number of metrics is expected to increase even further with the advent of cognitive radios that will allow unlicensed terminals to access underutilized portions of licensed spectrum. Each spectrum band will be thus subject not only to different propagation and load conditions, but also to different licensing, billing and pricing schemes. Therefore, new tools are required in the design of future wireless networks, which are able to handle simultaneously network and economic metrics.

1.2   Paper Objectives

This paper proposes the use of *multi-objective and financial portfolio optimization* tools for a trade-off analysis and optimization of a wireless carrier-sense multiple access (CSMA) protocol enabled with cooperative relaying diversity. Multi-objective optimization is the formal mathematical framework that addresses the simultaneous optimization of different and potentially competing objective functions [3]. Since this type of problem usually lacks a unique solution that simultaneously satisfies the individual optimality conditions of all targeted metrics, the concept of *Pareto optimality* is commonly employed. A Pareto optimal solution provides an optimal solution for a subset of the objective functions, i.e. it is not dominated by any other solution [3]. The number of Pareto solutions can be potentially infinite, thus describing a *Pareto frontier*. The objective functions of this multi-objective optimization problem can also include financial portfolio metrics such as *return* and *risk* (or variance of the return). Each network resource can be therefore considered also as a financial asset whose allocation will attempt to maximize return and minimize risk, similar to a financial stock market problem.

The system that will be subject to this multi-objective and financial portfolio optimization is a network with cooperative users. Inactive terminals that overheard the transmissions of other terminals in the network are allowed to relay to the base station (if necessary) copies of the original transmission [4]-[7]. All copies of the signal are appropriately combined at the destination, mimicking a macroscopic, virtual multiple antenna system. Cooperative relaying has gained attention over (or as complement of) other solutions such as distributed antenna systems or DAS (e.g., [8]), mainly because of the rapid and low cost potential deployment of relays. Cooperative diversity has shown interesting gains in the PHY-layer that makes it suitable for future networks. However, several issues remain open in the optimization, MAC-PHY cross-layer design and RRM integration for this type of systems [7]. This paper attempts to partially fill this gap by addressing a *trade-off design* of a CSMA protocol enabled with cooperation. The original protocol and reception model were proposed previously in [9] and [10], respectively. The analysis presented here is focused on different types of trade-off region: *throughput region, sum-throughput vs. fairness, sum-throughput vs. power, and return vs. risk regions.* The results shed light on the advantages of cooperation in terms of trade-off analysis between different metrics.

1.3   Related Works

Techno-economic analysis and study of wireless networks has been addressed extensively in the literature. The conventional approach is the use of a techno-economic model to evaluate the revenue of an operator under a given set of resource allocation assumptions. The main objective was to find the optimum resource allocation that provides the highest revenue and that satisfies users of the network [11]. In the context of cognitive radio, research in this area has been intensive over the last few years due to the relevance of opportunistic spectrum usage. A review of different approaches for the use of economic optimization tools in cognitive radio can be found in [12]. The authors have also proposed a market equilibrium approach where primary and secondary users implement a learning algorithm so that they can adapt accordingly the amount of spectrum used, the pricing and the optimum demand. Most of the existing works are based on game theoretic concepts (see [13]- [17]). The work in [16] has used an atomic congestion game theoretic approach in a wireless network with spatial reuse and inter-user interference. The work in [17] addresses the problem of calculating the optimum spectrum pricing in a dynamic spectrum market. Another related approach for the use of economics in cognitive radio can be found in works such as [18] and [19] and references therein, which are based on the concepts of auction theory.

This paper uses multi-objective portfolio optimization under the assumption that *each transmission is a financial asset.* Our work explicitly introduces the concept of risk in the resource allocation problem and derives relevant expressions that allow for its interpretation as a financial stock market problem. The work in [20] has used the concept of return and variance of the return in the context of spectrum pricing. Our approach is different from these previous works regarding the explicit use of multi-objective optimization and the exploration of the boundaries of different Pareto optimal frontiers. This allows us to visualize geometrical attributes and the potential trade-off between network and economic performance metrics. In other words, instead of searching a Nash or market equilibrium as in game theory, our contribution explicitly explores the boundaries of different trade-off performance regions. In this sense, our approach complements previous works in the literature by providing a framework for trade-off analysis and explicit interpretation of financial market stock tools in wireless networks.

The structure of this paper is as follows. Section 2 describes the proposed protocol. Section 3 describes the reception model for collision-free and cooperative (re)transmissions. Section 4 provides the definition of the performance metrics and the different trade-off regions. The boundaries of these trade-off regions are derived using multi-objective optimization in Section 5. Section 6 presents some performance results, and finally Section 7 presents the conclusions of the paper.

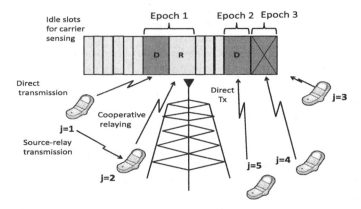

Fig. 1. Carrier-sense multiple access network with cooperative diversity

2   System Model and Protocol Description

Consider the slotted wireless random access network depicted in Fig. 1 with one base station (BS) and J user terminals. Each user j has a buffer that is assumed to have always packets ready to be transmitted (full queue or dominant system assumption). Transmissions will be controlled by a Bernoulli random process with parameter p_j, which is also the transmission probability of user j. All channels are independently and Rayleigh distributed with parameter σ_j for the link between user j and the BS, and with parameter $\sigma_j^{(k)}$ for the link between user j and user k. Users are allowed to cooperate with each other by relaying, if necessary, their signals towards the BS, where they are conveniently combined. The cooperative terminals will employ decode-and-forward (DF) relaying protocol. Since cooperation in half duplex systems requires more than one phase or time-slot, transmissions will be arranged in *periods or epoch-slots* with a variable length (in time- slots) denoted by the random variable l (see Fig. 1). At the beginning of an epoch-slot, each user senses the channel, and in case of being sensed as idle then the user starts the Bernoulli-distributed random transmission process. The packet length will be fixed to L *time-slots* or *packet-units*. This means that the carrier sensing is performed L times across the duration of a transmission. *Perfect carrier sensing* is assumed in all derivations [1]. All packet collisions are assumed to yield to the loss of all the transmitted information. However, whenever a collision-free transmission occurs, then all the inactive (non-contending) terminals and the BS will attempt to decode the signal. If the BS finds the packet as erroneous then it requests its retransmission from another terminal via an ideal feedback channel. This feedback channel has four possible outcomes $'0/1/e/r'$ which indicate, respectively, *idle* slot ($'0'$), *correct transmission* ($'1'$), *collision* ($'e'$), and *retransmission request* ($'r'$). If the feedback is $'r'$ then all the remaining idle terminals with a correct version of the original packet proceed

---

[1] Imperfect carrier-sensing can be regarded as a source of additional collisions in all derivations.

to relay a copy in the next time-slot with probability p_R. The BS stores all the received copies and uses maximum ratio combining (MRC) with a maximum of M branches (retransmissions plus the initial transmission) to improve packet reception. Each retransmission is requested if the reception process in previous transmissions has failed. In the illustrative example in Fig. 1, the small idle slots illustrate the granularity of carrier-sensing mechanism. The first active epoch is collision-free with terminal $j = 1$. Note that terminal $j = 2$ has received also the first transmission of terminal $j = 1$. However, the BS has not received the signal correctly and proceeds to request retransmission from terminal $j = 2$ in the next time slot. The second active epoch is also collision-free with terminal $j = 5$, but since the signal was correctly received by the BS, there is no cooperation. Finally, the third epoch experiences an unresolvable collision between terminals $j = 3$ and $j = 4$.

3   Packet Reception Model

This section has been provided in [9] and [10]. The results are summarized here for convenience and clarity in subsequent analysis. Consider that the instantaneous post-MRC processing SNR of user j at the BS during the nth time-slot of an epoch is denoted by $\gamma_{j,n}$. The correct reception probability of a packet of user j during the nth time-slot of an epoch, denoted by $q_{j,n}$, is given by the probability that the instantaneous SNR exceeds the reception threshold β [9][2]:

$$q_{j,n} = \Pr\{\gamma_{j,n} > \beta\} \tag{1}$$

Now consider that the instantaneous SNR of a transmission of user j experienced at the terminal of user k that will act as potential relay is denoted by $\gamma_j^{(k)}$ $(j \neq k)$. The correct reception probability of a packet of user j at relay k, denoted by $q_j^{(k)}$, is thus given by:

$$q_j^{(k)} = \Pr\{\gamma_j^{(k)} > \beta\}, ' \qquad j \neq k. \tag{2}$$

Since all channels are Rayleigh distributed, then the SNR values both at the destination and at the potential relays during the first time-slot of an epoch are exponentially distributed. The reception probabilities in (1) and (2) are thus given by the complementary cumulative distribution function (CCDF) of the exponential distribution $q_{j,1} = e^{-\beta/\widehat{\gamma}_{j,1}}$, and $q_j^{(k)} = e^{-\beta/\widehat{\gamma}_j^{(k)}}$, where $\widehat{\gamma}_{j,1} = E[\gamma_{j,1}] = \sigma_j^2$, $\widehat{\gamma}_j^{(k)} = E[\gamma_{j,k}] = \sigma_{j,k}^2$, and $E[\cdot]$ is the statistical average operator. Let us now address the modelling of the reception process during the cooperative phases. Since cooperative phases are activated only when the previous phases did not achieve the required SNR threshold, then it is relevant

---

[2] The SNR threshold reception model is commonly used in the literature to incorporate the effects of the PHY-layer into MAC-layer design. Therefore the instantaneous SNR is the quality indicator of the underlying channel and signal processing algorithms.

to study the statistics of reception conditional on the events in the preceeding time-slots. The cumulative distribution function of $\gamma_{j,n}$ conditional on the SNR of previous time slots being below β ($\gamma_{j,n-1} < \beta$) is given by (see [10] for details):

$$F_{\gamma_{j,n}|\gamma_{j,n-1}<\beta}(\gamma_{j,n}) = \frac{F_{\gamma_{j,n}}(\gamma_{j,n})}{F_{\gamma_{j,n-1}}(\beta)}, \quad j \neq k., \tag{3}$$

where $F_{\gamma_{j,n}}(\gamma_{j,n})$ is the unconditional CDF of the random variable $\gamma_{j,n}$ (see [10] for the analytic formula). Therefore, the reception probability during the nth time slot of an epoch given an incorrect packet reception in the previous $n-1$ transmissions is given by [10]:

$$q_{j,n|t_{j,n-1}=0} = 1 - F_{\gamma_{j,n}|\gamma_{j,n-1}<\beta}(\beta). \tag{4}$$

Details of these derivations can be found in [10].

4   Trade-Off Performance Regions

4.1   Throughput Region

Throughput can be defined as the ratio of the average number of correctly received *packet-units* per epoch-slot to the average length of an epoch-slot ($E[l]$). Considering that collisions yield the loss of all packets involved in the conflict, then a transmission of user j is free of collision with probability $p_j \prod_{k \neq j} \bar{p}_k$, where $\bar{a} = 1 - a$ is the complement to one of a, for any a (i.e.,$\bar{p}_j = 1 - p_j$). In addition, consider that $p_{s,j}$ is the correct reception probability of user j given that its transmission is collision-free and that cooperation is used. The throughput is thus given by:

$$T_j = \frac{L p_{s,j} p_j \prod_{k \neq j} \bar{p}_k}{E[l]}, \tag{5}$$

where the correct reception probability of user j in absence of collision can be otained by adding the contributions from all M possible cooperative stages:

$$p_{s,j} = q_{j,1} + \sum_{n=2}^{M} q_{j,n|t_{j,n-1}=0} \prod_{m=1}^{n-1} \bar{q}_{j,m|t_{j,m-1}=0}, \tag{6}$$

where $q_{j,m|t_{j,m-1}=0} = q_{j,1}$ when $m = 1$. The average length of an epoch-slot in the denominator of (5) can be obtained by considering all contributions of idle and busy epoch-slots: one time slot with probability $\prod_{k=1}^{J} \bar{p}_k$, at least L time-slots with probability $1 - \prod_{k=1}^{J} \bar{p}_k$, and more than L time-slots with probability $\sum_j p_j \prod_{k \neq j} \bar{p}_k$ weighted by $E[l_{c,j}]$, which denotes the average number of cooperative retransmissions for user j once a cooperative phase has been activated. The average length of an epoch can thus be written as:

$$E[l] = \sum_{j=1}^{J} L E[l_{c,j}] p_j \prod_{k \neq j} \bar{p}_k + L + \bar{L} \prod_{k=1}^{J} \bar{p}_k, \tag{7}$$

where $E[l_{c,j}] = \sum_{n=2}^{M}(n-1)q_{j,n|t_{j,n-1}=0}\prod_{m=1}^{n-1}\bar{q}_{j,m|t_{j,m-1}=0}$. is the summation of all contributions of the M possible cooperative stages. Let us now define the concept of throughput region. For this purpose, let $\mathbf{T} = [T_1, T_2, \ldots, T_J]^T$ be the vector of stacked throughput values of all terminals, and $\mathbf{p} = [p_1, p_2, \ldots, p_J]^T$ the vector of stacked transmission probabilities. The throughput region $\mathcal{C}_T$ is the union over all possible realizations of throughput values for all terminals and for all possible transmission policies ($0 \leq p_j \leq 1$) [21]:

$$\mathcal{C}_T = \{\tilde{\mathbf{T}}|\tilde{T}_j = T_j(p), 0 \leq p_j \leq 1\}, \tag{8}$$

which can be simply considered as the region of all achievable values of terminal throughput. The throughput region is the main performance metric used in the analysis of random access protocols in asymmetrical settings [21].

4.2 Sum-Throughput vs. Fairness Region

The sum-throughput can be defined as follows:

$$T = \sum_{j=1}^{J} T_j. \tag{9}$$

Fairness will be evaluated in this paper by means of the Gini-index, which is commonly used in the area of economics to measure income inequality [25]. The Gini-index can be defined mathematically as follows [25]:

$$F_G = \frac{\sum_{j=1}^{M}\sum_{k=1}^{J}|T_j - T_k|}{2J^2\mu}, \tag{10}$$

where $\mu = \sum_{j=1}^{J} T_j/J$ is the mean value. A value of Gini-index of zero indicates the best fairness scenario where the users have identical statistical performance. A value of F_G equal to one is the worst fairness scenario as only one user overtakes all the resources of the network. For convenience in subsequent analysis, (10) can be rewritten as follows: $F_G = \frac{\sum_{j=1}^{J}\sum_{k=1}^{J} a_{j,k}(T_j-T_k)}{2JT} = \frac{X}{2JT}$ where $a_{j,k}$ is defined as $a_{j,k} = \begin{cases} 1, & T_j \geq T_k \\ -1, & T_j < T_k \end{cases}$. Consider the vector $\mathbf{F} = [T \quad F_G]^T$ of stacked values of sum-throughput and fairness. The sum-throughput vs. fairness trade-off region can be defined as the union of all achievable values $[T \quad F_G]$ for all possible transmission policies ($0 \leq p_j \leq 1$):

$$\mathcal{C}_F = \{\tilde{\mathbf{F}}|\tilde{T} = T(\mathbf{p}), \tilde{F}_G = F_G(\mathbf{p}), 0 \leq p_j \leq 1\}. \tag{11}$$

4.3   Sum-Throughput vs. Transmit Power Region

In this paper, average transmit power will be considered as proportional to the transmit rate of the system plus the potential cooperative retransmissions. Therefore, in our setting, we can define the average consumed power as follows:

$$P = \alpha \sum_{j=1}^{J} p_j \left(1 + \prod_{k \neq j} \bar{p}_k E[l_{c,j}]\right), \tag{12}$$

where α is a proportionality constant. Having defined both sum-throughput and transmit power consumption, let us now define the concept of sum throughput vs. power trade-off region. First, we define the vector $\mathbf{P} = [T \quad P]^T$ of stacked values of sum-throughput and power. The sum-throughput vs. power trade-off region can be defined as the union of all achievable values $[T P]$ for all possible transmission policies ($0 \leq p_j \leq 1$):

$$\mathcal{C}_P = \{\tilde{\mathbf{P}} | \tilde{T} = T(\mathbf{p}), \tilde{P} = P(\mathbf{p}), 0 \leq p_j \leq 1\}. \tag{13}$$

4.4   Return vs. Risk Trade-Off Region

Let us define the instantaneous return per correctly transmitted packet of user j as r_j, and the average return as $E[r_j] = \hat{r}_j$. The instantaneous return of the network per epoch-slot can be thus written as follows:

$$R = \sum_{j=1}^{J} r_j t_j, \tag{14}$$

where t_j is the binary random variable that indicates whether a packet transmission was correct or not per epoch-slot. The average return can be thus defined as the ratio of the average return per epoch-slot to the the average length of an epoch-slot:

$$\hat{R} = \frac{E[R]}{E[l]} = \sum_{j=1}^{J} \hat{r}_j T_j. \tag{15}$$

Let us now calculate the average risk as the ratio of the variance of the instantaneous return per epoch to the average length of an epoch:

$$S = \frac{E[R^2] - E[R]^2}{E[l]} = \frac{E[R^2]}{E[l]} - E[l]\hat{R}^2 = \frac{\sum_{j=1}^{J} E[r_j^2]}{E[l]} - E[l]\hat{R}^2 \tag{16}$$

Consider the vector $\mathbf{R} = [\hat{R} \quad S]^T$ of stacked values of return and risk. The return vs. risk trade-off region can be defined as the union of all achievable values $[\hat{R} \quad S]$ for all possible transmission policies ($0 \leq p_j \leq 1$) :

$$\mathcal{C}_R = \{\tilde{\mathbf{R}} | \tilde{R} = R(\mathbf{p}), \tilde{S} = S(\mathbf{p}), 0 \leq p_j \leq 1\}. \tag{17}$$

5 Multi-objective Optimization

To obtain the envelope of the trade-off regions, a multi-objective optimization of I functions F_i is here proposed:

$$\mathbf{P}_{opt} = \arg\max_{\mathbf{P}} \quad [F_1, F_2 \quad \dots F_i, \dots \quad F_I]. \tag{18}$$

Since this vector optimization usually lacks a unique solution [3], the concept of Pareto optimal trade-off front is commonly employed. A Pareto optimal solution can be loosely defined here as the point that is at least optimum for one or more of the elements of the vector objective function $[F_1, F_2 \quad \dots \quad F_I]$, or in other words when none of the objective functions can be improved in value without degrading some of the other objective values (see [3] for a complete definition). The multi-objective optimization problem can be transformed into a single objective optimization problem using the method of scalarization [3]:

$$\mathbf{P}_{opt} = \arg\max_{\mathbf{P}} \sum_i \mu_i F_i, \tag{19}$$

where μ_i is the relative weight given to the ith objective function. Differentiating the objective function in (19) we obtain a set of equations given by $\sum_i \mu_i \frac{\partial F_i}{\partial p_k} = 0$, $k = 1.., J$. Assuming $J = I$, the solution of a subset $\mathcal{S}_o$ of I of these linear equations independent from the values of the weighting factors μ_k can be proved, in our context, to be equivalent to setting the following Jacobian determinant to zero [23] [22]:

$$|\mathbf{J}_o| = 0, \tag{20}$$

where $J_o(k, i) = \frac{\partial F_i}{\partial p_k}$ is the (i, k) entry of the Jacobian matrix $\mathbf{J}_o$, $k \in \mathcal{S}_o$. The final solution is given by the union of the solutions for all the possible selections of equations $\mathcal{S}_o$.

5.1 Throughput Region

In the case of the throughput region, the $I = J$ objective functions to be optimized in (19) are the throughput functions of each terminal: $F_j = T_j$, $j = 1, \dots, J$. This means that the elements of the Jacobian determinant in (20) are given by $J_{k,j} = \frac{\partial T_k}{\partial p_j}$. In this case, the number of objective functions is equivalent to the number of variables of the optimization. The final expression is given by (see [9] for details of the derivation):

$$\sum_{j=1}^{J} L p_j = L + \bar{L} \prod_{j=1}^{J} \bar{p}_j. \tag{21}$$

This last expression together with the expression for the throughput of the different users in (5) characterize the boundary of the throughput region.

5.2   Sum-Throughput vs. Fairness

In the case of the sum-throughput vs. fairness, the $I = 2$ objective functions to be optimized are $F_1 = T$ in (5) and $F_2 = F_G$ in (10). Therefore, the Jacobian determinant in (20) reduces to:

$$\frac{\partial X}{\partial p_k} \frac{\partial T}{\partial p_j} = \frac{\partial X}{\partial p_j} \frac{\partial T}{\partial p_k}, \quad j \neq k, \quad j, k \in \{1, \dots, J\}. \tag{22}$$

In the particular case of two users $J = 2$ the previous expression can be proved to be equivalent to the Jacobian of the throughput region and thus boil down to the solution in (21). Further details are provided in the section of results.

5.3   Sum-Throughput vs. Transmit Power Region

In the case of the sum-throughput vs. power, the $I = 2$ objective functions to be optimized are $F_1 = T$ in (5) and $F_2 = P$ in (12). Therefore, the Jacobian determinant in (20) reduces to

$$\begin{vmatrix} \frac{\partial P}{\partial p_j} & \frac{\partial P}{\partial p_k} \\ \frac{\partial T}{\partial p_j} & \frac{\partial T}{\partial p_k} \end{vmatrix} = 0, \quad j \neq k, \quad j, k \in \{1, \dots, J\}. \tag{23}$$

This expression can be solved via numerical methods based on steepest gradient descent tools.

5.4   Return vs. Risk

In the case of the return vs. risk trade-off region, the $I = 2$ objective functions to be optimized are $F_1 = R$ in (15) and $F_2 = S$ in (16). Therefore, the Jacobian determinant in (20) becomes:

$$\begin{vmatrix} \frac{\partial \hat{R}}{\partial p_j} & \frac{\partial S}{\partial p_k} \\ \frac{\partial \hat{R}}{\partial p_j} & \frac{\partial S}{\partial p_k} \end{vmatrix} = 0, \quad j \neq k, \quad j, k \in \{1, \dots, J\}. \tag{24}$$

This expression can be solved via numerical methods based on steepest gradient descent tools.

6   Results

This section presents the graphical results of the analytic work presented in previous sections. For convenience, all results assume a system with $J = 2$ users. All the results can be extended to a multi-user scenario. User 1 will be modelled with low reception probabilities using a parameter $\hat{\gamma}_{1,1} = 1$, while the second user will experience high values of reception probabilities with parameter $\hat{\gamma}_{2,1} = 10$.

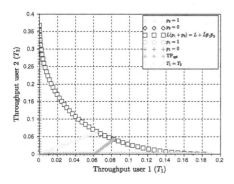

Fig. 2. Throughput region for $L = 1$ and $M = 1$

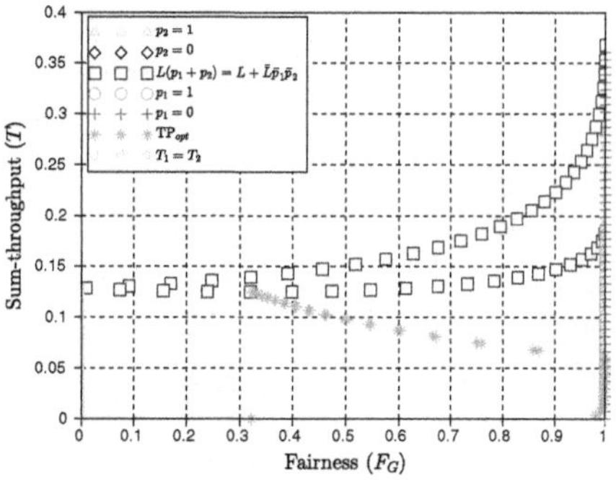

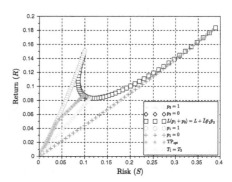

Fig. 3. Sum-throughput (T) vs. fairness (F_G) region for $L = 1$ and $M = 1$

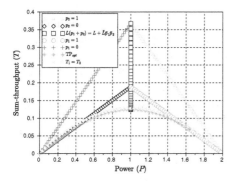

Fig. 4. Sum-throughput (T) vs. Tx. power (P) region for $L = 1$ and $M = 1$

Fig. 5. Return ($\hat{R}$) vs. risk (S) region for $L = 1$ and $M = 1$

User-to-user communication is implemented with parameter $\hat{\gamma}_1^{(2)} = \hat{\gamma}_2^{(1)} = 8$. The reception threshold is set to $\beta = 1$. In terms of financial parameters, we selected $\hat{r}_1 = 0.8$, $\hat{r}_2 = 0.5$, $E[r_1^2] = 0.01$, and $E[r_2^2] = 0.9$. While this is a rather arbitrary selection of financial parameters, it is possible to obtain some useful results and conclusions for the general case.

Fig. 2 to Fig. 5 present the sketches of different trade-off regions for the case of $L = 1$ and $M = 1$, which is a random access protocol without carrier-sensing (ALOHA) and without cooperative diversity. All the figures contain the envelopes of the different trade-off regions obtained from multi-objective optimization, relevant boundary conditions (e.g. $p = 0$, $p = 1$), and also the projections of the boundaries(envelopes) of the other regions under analysis. Fig. 2 shows the throughput region, where we can observe it is non-convex due to the collision model and the ALOHA protocol operation. The boundary described by the Pareto solution is labelled as $L(p_1 + p_2) = L + \bar{L}\bar{p}_1\bar{p}_2$ which is the expression

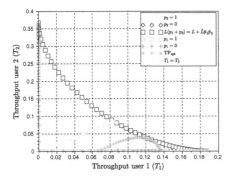
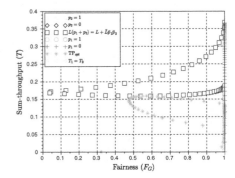

Fig. 6. Throughput region for $L = 4$ and $M = 1$

Fig. 7. Sum-throughput (T) vs. fairness (F_G) region for $L = 4$ and $M = 1$

in (21) for a two-user system. The projections of the Pareto optimal throughput-power envelope (labelled TP$_{opt}$) and the equal throughput curve (labelled $T_1 = T_2$) are also displayed. The non-convexity of the throughput region means that the trade-off region of sum-throughput and fairness region in Fig. 3 exhibits a rapid decrease of throughput for increasingly improving values of Gini-index (a value of zero indicates the best fairness condition). Note also that the boundary of the fairness region is described by half of the solution that describes the throughput region, which is the half corresponding to the user with best channel conditions. The other half is also displayed inside the region in Fig. 3. The sum-throughput vs. power trade-off region displayed in Fig. 4 shows that the region is defined by boundary conditions and by the Pareto solution in (23), which also describes the minimum sum-throughput curve. Note that the Pareto front of the throughput region labelled as $L(p_1 + p_2) = L + \bar{L}\bar{p}_1\bar{p}_2$ is projected as a vertical constant power line that cuts the region into two equal halves. The return vs. risk trade-off region displayed in Fig.5 is defined by boundary conditions with the point of maximum and minimum risk. The curve that defines the Pareto solution for the throughput and fairness region also describes the Pareto solution of the return vs. risk region by joining the points of maximum or minimum return (or risk). The non-convexity of the throughput region makes the return vs. risk region also non-convex, which means it is difficult to achieve high values of return without compromising risk and also fairness.

Fig. 6 and Fig.7 show, respectively, the throughput and sum-throughput vs. fairness trade-off regions for the case of $L = 4$ and $M = 1$, which is a carrier-sensing algorithm without cooperation. We can observe that the throughput region has become less non-convex, which leads to an increase of its area. This improvement on the convexity of the region can be also observed in a reduction of the steepness of the fairness Pareto curve in Fig. 7, which means that an improvement on fairness (reduction of Gini-index) does not yield a large drop of sum-throughput as in the case of ALOHA discussed previously in Fig 2 to Fig. 5.

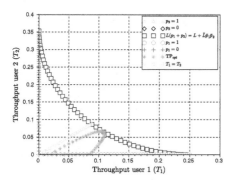

Fig. 8. Throughput region for $L = 1$ and $M = 4$

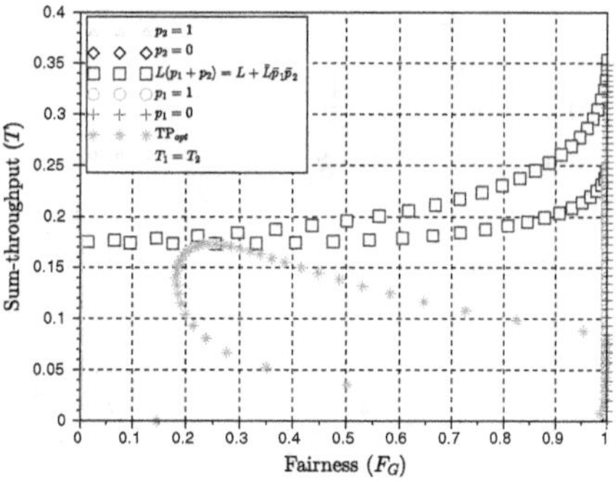

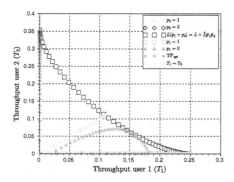

Fig. 10. Throughput region for $L = 4$ and $M = 4$

Fig. 9. Sum-throughput (T) vs. fairness (F_G) for $L = 1$ and $M = 4$

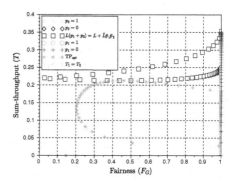

Fig. 11. Sum-throughput (T) vs. fairness (F_G) region for $L = 4$ and $M = 4$

Fig. 8 and Fig. 9 show, respectively, the throughput and sum-throughput vs. fairness trade-off regions for the case of $L = 1$ and $M = 4$, which is an ALOHA protocol enabled with cooperative diversity. We can observe that the throughput region has become less non-convex, but not as much as in the previous case with carrier-sensing, also yielding an increase of its area. We can observe that the increase of the area due to cooperation is mainly due to the improvement of the reception probabilities, which makes the user with the lower reception probability take benefit from the improved relaying capabilities. Note that, unlike the case of pure carrier-sensing displayed in Fig. 6 the region displayed in Fig. 8 with cooperation provides an effective improvement of the reception probability, particularly for user 1, shifting the area slightly towards the right hand side of the figure. By contrast, carrier sensing seems to improve the region mainly at the middle of the trade-off boundary region, which is the zone dominated by collisions. From these observations we can therefore conclude that both carrier sensing and cooperation yield useful

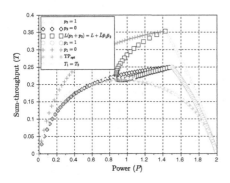

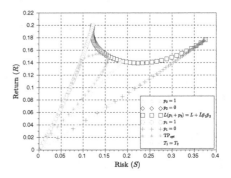

Fig. 12. Sum-throughput (T) vs. Tx. power (P).

Fig. 13. Return ($\hat{R}$) vs. risk (S).

improvements on the operation of the protocol under different networking circumstances: carrier sensing improves the avoidance of collisions, while cooperation improves the effective reception capabilities of the system. This improvement on the convexity of the region can be also observed in a reduction of the steepness of the fairness Pareto curve in Fig. 9, which means that an improvement on fairness (reduction of Gini index) is not accompanied by a considerable decline of aggregate throughput.

Fig. 10 to Fig. 13 show the results for a system with $L = 4$ and $M = 4$ combining the benefits from carrier-sensing and cooperation. Observe that the throughput region is considerably increased with a less non-convex shape, which is the result of improved collision management with carrier sensing and also improved reception probability due to cooperative relaying. These improvements are also translated into a better trade-off between fairness and sum-throughput which are shown as a more flat curve in Fig. 11. Higher values of sum-throughput can be achieved without sacrificing too much fairness between users. In terms of power consumption we can observe in Fig. 12 that power consumption has been considerably increased in comparison to the ALOHA case without cooperation. However, we can observe that the increase of power consumption along the curve labelled with $L(p_1 + p_2) = L + \bar{L}\bar{p}_1\bar{p}_2$ is mainly for the case where one of the users transmits while the other user is idle, and that even power reduction can be observed in the region where both users start contending with each other. Therefore, we can conclude that cooperation and carrier-sensing can achieve good levels of sum-throughput without compromising too much consumed power and fairness. In terms of financial performance we can observe in Fig. 13 that higher levels of return can be achieved with a good level of risk, in comparison with previous result in Fig. 5. This means that risk has been effectively reduced by means of cooperation and carrier-sensing.

7   Conclusions

This paper has presented the MAC-PHY cross-layer design of a class of carrier-sense multiple access protocol where users with good channel states can cooperate with users with bad channel states by relaying a copy of collision-free signals. Different types of trade-off region were here analysed by means of multi-objective and financial convex optimization tools. It was confirmed that cooperation provides an improvement of the reception capabilities of the system, particularly for users with bad channels states which benefit from users with better channel states relaying their signals towards the base station, where they were conveniently combined. This improved reception was translated in an increase of the throughput region, reduced steepness of the Pareto curve of sum-throughput vs. fairness and a better trade-off between return and risk in the network. In terms of power consumption, cooperation provides a considerable increase but in combination with carrier sensing was proved to yield a good compromise between network performance and consume power. Carrier-sensing was proved to reduce the non-convexity of the throughput region particularly when both users contend for the channel, which is also translated in a better trade-off between sum-throughput and fairness. In combination with cooperative diversity, carrier-sensing provides a considerable increase also in terms of the throughput region of the algorithm. Future work includes the use of multi-objective and financial optimization tools in the analysis of more complex random access schemes.

Acknowledgments. The research leading to these results has received funding from the ARTEMIS Joint Undertaking under grant agreement no. 621353, the Portuguese National Science Foundation FCT, and by the North Portugal Regional Operational Programme (ON.2 O Novo Norte), under the National Strategic Reference Framework (NSRF), through the European Regional Development Fund (ERDF), and by FCT, within project ref. NORTE-07-0124-FEDER-000063 (BEST-CASE, New Frontiers).

References

1. Srivastaya, V., Montani, M.: Cross-layer design: a survey and the road ahead. IEEE Commun. Ma. **43**(12), 112–119 (2005)
2. Samano-Robles, R., Gameiro, A.: Network and Economic Trade-off Performance Regions of Cognitive Radio Systems with Transmit Power Control. Applied Mathematics and Information Science **7**(5), 1755–1766 (2013)
3. Boyd, S., Vandenberghe, L.: Convex optimization. Cambridge University Press (2004)
4. Chen, W., Dai, L., Letaief, K.B., Cao, Z.: A unified cross-layer framework for resource allocation in cooperative networks. IEEE Transactions on Wireless Commun. **7**(8), 3000–3012 (2008)
5. Zhou, Y., Liu, J., Zhai, C., Zheng, L.: Two-transmitter two-receiver Cooperative MAC protocol: cross-layer design and performance analaysis. IEEE Trans. on Vehicular Tech. **59**(8), 4116–27 (2010)

6. Liu, P., Tao, Z., Lin, Z., Erkip, E., Panwar, S.: Cooperative wireless communications: a cross-layer approach. IEEE Wireless Communications Magazine **13**(4), 84–92 (2006)
7. Scaglione, A., Goeckel, D.L., Laneman, J.N.: Cooperative communications in mobile ad hoc networks. IEEE Signal Processing Magazine **23**(5), 18–29 (2006)
8. Choi, W., Andrews, J.G.: Downlink performance and capacity of distributed antenna systems in a multicell environment. IEEE Transactions on Wireless Communications **6**(1), 69–73 (2007)
9. Samano-Robles, R., Gameiro, A.: Throughput, Stability, and Fairness of Carrier Sense Multiple Access with Cooperative Diversity. International Journal of Communications **3**, 21–31. http://www.seipub.org/ijc/Download.aspx?ID=9051
10. Samano-Robles, R., Gameiro, A.: A packet reception model for cooperative diversity in wireless multi-cell networks. In: International Conference on Consumer Electronics, Berlin, Germany, September 2011
11. Smura, T.: Techno-economic modelling of wireless network and industry architectures, Doctoral dissertation. Aalto University (2012)
12. Niyato, D., Hossain, E.: Spectrum trading in cognitive radio networks: A market-equilibrium-based approach. IEEE Wireless Communications **15**, 71–80 (2008)
13. Southwell, R., Chen, X., Huang, J.: Quality of service satisfaction games for spectrum sharing. In: IEEE INFOCOM - Mini Conference, Turin, Italy (2013)
14. Chen, X., Huang, J.: Spatial spectrum access game: nash equilibria and distributed learning. In: ACM Mobihoc, Hilton Head Island, South Carolina (2012)
15. Duan, L., Huang, J., Shou, B.: Duopoly Competition in Dynamic Spectrum Leasing and Pricing. IEEE Transactions on Mobile Computing **11**, 1706–1719 (2012)
16. Tekin, C., et al.: Atomic Congestion Games on Graphs and Their Applications in Networking. IEEE Transactions on Networking **20**, 1541–1552 (2012)
17. Duan, L., Huang, J., Shou, B.: Investment and Pricing with Spectrum Uncertainty: A Cognitive Operators Perspective. IEEE Transactions on Mobile Computing **10**, 1590–1604 (2011)
18. Zhang, Y., Niyato, D., Wang, P., Hossain, E.: Auction-based resource allocation in cognitive radio systems. IEEE Communications Magazine **50**, 108–120 (2008)
19. Huang, J., Berry, R., Honig, M.L.: Auction-based Spectrum Sharing. Springer Journal Mobile Networks and Applications **11**, 405–408 (2006)
20. Wysocki, T.A., Jamalipour, A.: An Economic Welfare Preserving Framework for Spot Pricing and Hedging of Spectrum Rights for Cognitive Radio. IEEE Transactions on Network and Service Management **9**, 87–99 (2012)
21. Luo, J., Ephremides, A.: On the throughput, capacity, and stability regions of random multiple access. IEEE Transactions on Information Theory **52**(6), 2593–2607 (2006)
22. Samano-Robles, R., Ghogho, M., McLernon, D.C.: Wireless Networks with retransmission diversity and carrier sense multiple access. IEEE Transactions on Signal Processing **57**(9), 3722–3726 (2009)
23. Abramson, N.: The throughput of packet broadcasting channels. IEEE Transactions on Communications **25**(1), 117–128 (1977)
24. Tobagi, F., Kleinrock, L.: Packet switching in radio channels: part IV-stability considerations and dynamic control in carrier sense multiple access. IEEE Transactions on Communications **25**(10), 1103–1119 (1977)
25. Marshall, A.W., Olkin, I.: Inequalities: theory of majorization and its applications. Acaemic Press (1979)

A Centralized Mechanism to Make Predictions Based on Data from Multiple WSNs

Gabriel Martins Dias[(✉)], Simon Oechsner, and Boris Bellalta

Department of Information and Communication Technologies,
Pompeu Fabra University, Barcelona, Spain
gabriel.martins@upf.edu

Abstract. In this work, we present a method that exploits a scenario with inter-Wireless Sensor Networks (WSNs) information exchange by making predictions and adapting the workload of a WSN according to their outcomes. We show the feasibility of an approach that intelligently utilizes information produced by other WSNs that may or not belong to the same administrative domain. To illustrate how the predictions using data from external WSNs can be utilized, a specific use-case is considered, where the operation of a WSN measuring relative humidity is optimized using the data obtained from a WSN measuring temperature. Based on a dedicated performance score, the simulation results show that this new approach can find the optimal operating point associated to the trade-off between energy consumption and quality of measurements. Moreover, we outline the additional challenges that need to be overcome, and draw conclusions to guide the future work in this field.

1 Introduction

Nowadays, forests, cities and houses, among others, are monitored by multiple Wireless Sensor Networks (WSNs) that may belong to different organizations, both public and private, as well as to individual citizens. In addition, there is a high heterogeneity regarding the technologies, protocols and standards used in WSNs. In this situation, each WSN usually operates completely independent of other WSNs, even if they are covering the same physical area, and is thus not able to take any advantage of the presence of those other WSNs to enrich its collected data nor to optimize its operation.

However, WSN performance can be improved by combining data generated from different sensors, belonging to the same node, other nodes from the same network or from other WSNs. This data sharing allows each WSN to build a deeper knowledge about its surroundings, may reduce the probability of getting wrong values and taking wrong decisions, and encompasses wider areas and different perspectives of the same environment.

In an era of high availability of data from the cloud, we are interested in using data from other WSNs to reduce the energy consumption and improve the quality of the measurements done by a target WSN. The external information will be used to make predictions and change the operation of the nodes and

© Springer International Publishing Switzerland 2015
M. Jonsson et al. (Eds.): MACOM 2015, LNCS 9305, pp. 19–32, 2015.
DOI: 10.1007/978-3-319-23440-3_2

save energy when the environmental conditions do not indicate that big changes will happen in the near future. For example, relative humidity and temperature values usually have a high correlation, and the former may have a higher variation if the latter is changing.

This paper lists some of the existing alternatives for collaboration and prediction in WSNs and develops further the inter-WSNs information exchange concept introduced in [1] and in [2]. The main idea behind the inter-WSN information exchange is that the data gathered by other WSNs can be exchanged via their sinks and used to improve the operation of the target one, and vice versa. Our main contribution is a mechanism that uses the data from collaborating WSNs to make predictions. In order to validate our idea, we show how the WSNs evolve using this kind of collaboration, define a way to scale the quality of the measurements and the WSNs' performance, and finally present some simulation results from a chosen scenario consisting of two WSNs, one for monitoring the relative humidity and another for the temperature. Based on the presented results, we show how energy-efficient and accurate it can be.

The paper is organized in the following sections: In Section 2, we describe related works about collaboration between WSNs, the use of data from external sensors and predictions in WSN environments; the details of our proposed mechanism are explained in Section 3; the use case considered for the tests is detailed in Section 4; the simulation results and the evaluation of the approach are explained in Section 5 and; at the end, our conclusions and ideas for future work are shown in Section 6.

2   Related Work

A system that combines the action of individual components may produce better results than the individual components acting separately. Supported by this premisse, several collaboration mechanisms in WSNs have been developed. Most of the approaches explore the collaboration between sensor nodes of the same WSN. In contrast to them, we extend the concept of collaboration to an upper layer and build the information exchange between different WSNs, without losing any other possible collaboration from the other levels.

An inter-domain routing protocol is described in [3], where it is shown that the gateways may share information about their nodes and take advantage of being physically close to each other. This information can be used to transmit packets through nodes of the other WSNs and can be done either to share the information or for routing purposes. Even though the idea of our work is to create a link between nodes from different WSNs, it is neither meant to share resources nor information between wireless sensor nodes, but the knowledge that the network is able to produce based on collected data.

In [4], the authors describe a scenario where a system is responsible for building a richer knowledge about the environment by making use of the information produced by other WSNs. In their example, wireless sensor nodes combine sensory information with their localization and help other systems to localize and track objects from a distance. The goal of the described approach is to enable a robot to use the data retrieved by a WSN that detects the presence of objects inside the monitored area. After receiving the information from the WSN, the robot interprets the position of the object and moves itself to its location in order to get more details about the real situation. Their approach is different from ours mainly because it uses a non-generic solution that is highly coupled to the presented scenario without a WSN as the beneficiary of the collected information, besides not making any prediction with the information received from the others.

Besides the works that encourage the collaboration among WSNs, some authors applied predictions in order to reduce the energy consumption in the WSNs and extend their lifetime. In [5], the authors developed an algorithm for WSN applications that require a continuous delivery of sensor measurements, such as temperature and traffic monitoring. In order to build sets of nodes that provide trustful measurements, it considers that a sensor measurement is predictable if the predicted value (on average) differs on less than a (user) defined threshold when using other nodes' measurements. After defining which sensors can be predicted by which other, the base station must find a set of subsets of active nodes such that a different prediction subset is used at each time, and such that all sensors are queried at least once during a cycle. After building this set, the base station must activate a subset of nodes at a time. In other words, only the sensor nodes from the active subset are activated during a time interval and all the others have their radios and sensors turned off in order to save energy and extend the WSN lifetime. Simulations using real data show that such approach can successfully achieve its goals depending on the user requirements and on the quality of the data. Similarly, our mechanism also assumes the task of selecting which sensors are going to be active in the next time interval. However, our mechanism is able to react to environmental changes, while their work is less dynamic. That is, once the sets of sensors are defined, they will be interleaved independently of changes that may happen around the WSN. We highlight that it may be possible to improve our mechanism by adopting their techniques to build the groups of sensors in a way that there is no reduction in the quality of the measurements and the energy savings are maximized.

The solution presented in [6] (called BBQ) is a centralized mechanism used to query data based on sensor models. It assumes that the costs of retrieving data from many nodes can be extremely high and that sensors in close proximity are likely to have correlated readings, which may mean that most of the data provides little benefit in the quality of the answers given to the user. In order to save energy, the BBQ incorporates statistical models of real-world processes into the query processing architecture and acquires data from the sensors only when the model itself is not sufficiently rich to answer the query with acceptable confidence. To achieve such a goal, the BBQ approximates the probability density function of the measurements to multivariate Gaussian distributions and, given the correlation between the known measurement(s) and the unknown one(s), it calculates their expected value associated to a confidence interval. If the confidence level is greater or equal than a chosen threshold, it assumes that such value satisfies the system requirements. Otherwise, it calculates the energy consumed to retrieve new measurements considering the costs to activate the corresponding sensor and, finally, builds a query that will require the lowest energy consumption for the WSN and will give at least the minimum level of confidence set by the user. Similarly to our mechanism, it exploits the correlation between different types of data that the sensor nodes may be able to measure, for example, their own voltage and the local temperature. The difference from our work is that they do not provide a method to measure the quality of the measurements and the performance of the system.

3 Proposed Mechanism

Our system architecture is ready to use information from external WSNs, as described in [1] and [7]. To achieve the goal of optimizing the performance of the WSNs, they must be interconnected through their respective Enhanced Gateways (EGs). We explain the details of the mechanism in the following.

3.1 Centralized Decisions

Periodically, the data retrieved by the nodes are transmitted to the sink. After receiving all the measurements, the sink computes the received values before reporting them to the EG, which may forward them to external WSNs. In parallel, the EG may also receive information from external WSNs and, up to this point, all the data are collected and stored for further analysis. In intervals, the EG uses the collected data to predict if there will be changes in the near future. Figure 1 describes the possible states of a WSN.

The predictions done by the EG can have two different outcomes: *positive*, when changes in the environment are expected; and *negative*, otherwise. If an EG receives information from internal and external sources, each prediction may be based on a different data type and independent for each metric. In such cases, they can be combined in order to produce only one outcome. The outcomes can be compared with the real observations in order to verify the performance of the predictions. The feedback can be incorporated by the EG$_s$ in order to improve their future decisions.

3.2 Applications

Based on the outcome of its prediction, a EG selects the new strategy that the WSN must follow and will be applied by the sink. At the end, the sink transmits to its nodes a new configuration that they must follow in the next time interval, which may be an instruction to (de)activate themselves or to change the sensing intervals:

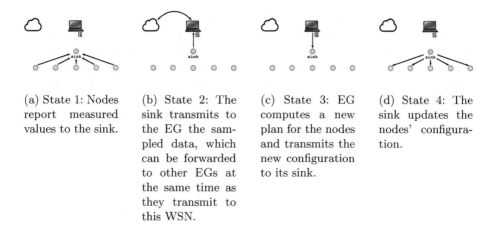

(a) State 1: Nodes report measured values to the sink.

(b) State 2: The sink transmits to the EG the sampled data, which can be forwarded to other EGs at the same time as they transmit to this WSN.

(c) State 3: EG computes a new plan for the nodes and transmits the new configuration to its sink.

(d) State 4: The sink updates the nodes' configuration.

Fig. 1. Different states of a WSNs using inter-WSN information exchange

Adaptive Sensor Nodes Selection. This application reduces the energy consumption of the network by deactivating some nodes during a certain period of time. In other words, when a node is deactivated, it does not make any measurement, but it may forward messages exchanged by their neighbors. We recall that the sets of active nodes can follow the guidelines described in [5], so the energy savings can be maximized without compromising the quality of the measurements.

Adaptive Sampling. Differently from the other application, this solution does not change the number of active nodes. However, when the EG has a *positive* outcome and changes are expected in the environment, the nodes should reduce the time between two consecutive measurement transmissions, consuming more energy and producing more information about the environment. Otherwise, the energy can be saved, because it is not expected big changes in the environment.

3.3 Quality of Measurements (QoM)

As explained before, one of the goals of this mechanism is to reduce the energy consumed in a WSN without reducing the QoM (i.e., a parameter that evaluates if the gathered information from the environment during a certain period is enough to accurately represent it). However, the level of the QoM depends on the type of information reported by the nodes.

We consider monitoring WSNs that make continuous transmissions to the sink and tolerate a small number of packet losses as well as delays between consecutive transmissions, but do not allow the reduction of the covered area because it might miss changes occurring in certain subareas. Therefore, we scaled the QoM as shown in Table 1. There, each interval with a *positive* outcome should be covered by more reports, increasing the level of knowledge about the environment. Although a high number of measurements always represents a *good*

QoM, the intervals with a *negative* observation can be covered by less reports without compromising the quality, thereby saving energy. Periods with a *negative* observation that are wrongly predicted mean that the system expected to have a *positive* observation in them, produced more measurements and, thus, wasted energy. Differently from the states that a *positive* is observed and the WSN produced a low number of measurements, those periods still have a *good* QoM, but the energy consumption might have been reduced and the WSN lifetime increased.

Table 1. Definition of QoM

		Prediction outcome	
		positive	*negative*
Actual observation	*positive*	GOOD	BAD
	negative	GOOD	GOOD

Based on this, the accuracy was defined as the percentage of intervals in a day in which the system was operating in a highlighted state. Moreover, the accuracy of *positives* is the percentage of intervals with *positives* covered by a high number of measurements.

Regarding the system operation, during intervals in which variations are predicted and the predictions have *positive* outcomes, the EG updates the operation of its WSN in order to collect more information. Each update on its operation affects either the number of active nodes or the time interval between two measurements done by the sensors. As a consequence of this, the number of measurements, the number of transmissions and the energy consumption have higher values during these periods of time, while the opposite effect occurs when no variation is predicted.

3.4 Performance Score

In order to evaluate how efficient the use of external information can be, we developed a way to compare the approaches. For a given scenario, we calculate the lowest energy consumption that the WSN may have ($E_{\min}$), which can be done by always setting the plan that produces less measurements during a day. On the other hand, we measure how much energy is consumed by the WSN when it produces the maximum number of measurements during the same time interval ($E_{\max}$). Thus, the percentage of energy saved by an approach (E_{ps}) is derived from the energy consumed ($E_{consumed}$) by the relation:

$$E_{ps} = \frac{E_{\max} - E_{consumed}}{E_{\max} - E_{\min}} \tag{1}$$

A correct prediction about a *negative* observation means that the system is producing less measurements and saving energy. Therefore, this accuracy factor is implicitly inserted in the value of E_{ps} and should not be considered again in the final equation. Considering this, the trade-off between the QoM and the energy consumption can be calculated if we use only the percentage of predictions of *positive* outcomes($P_{high\Delta}$) that the system could successfully do:

$$P_{high\Delta} = \frac{\# \text{ of positives correctly predicted}}{\# \text{ of observed positives}} \tag{2}$$

Finally, the *Performance score (p)* is defined as the product between the percentage of saved energy and the percentage of *positives* correctly predicted, which quantifies how much the system actually consumes to have such level of accuracy. If interpreted as a dot product between two vectors, the highest value represents the system having the highest possible energy savings and the highest possible accuracy *highΔs*:

$$p_{(\alpha)} = E_{ps}{}^{\alpha} \cdot P_{high\Delta}{}^{(1-\alpha)} \tag{3}$$

where $0 \leq \alpha \leq 1$ is the exponent that represents the system's priority on the energy saved over its accuracy. For example, if $\alpha < 0.5$, the energy savings will have a bigger impact at the performance score. Obviously, if $\alpha = 0.5$, the system will not prioritize any of them.

4   Use Case

To create a realistic use case, we used the temperature and relative humidity of 16 days measured by three different nodes in the experiments done in [5]. The simulated use case is based on a real scenario from where the data was fetched: an office with two WSNs deployed close to each other. There, nodes are positioned in a grid topology with two different WSNs: *Network A* monitoring temperature and *Network B* monitoring relative humidity.

Network A has one node that retrieves data from the environment, and a sink node that receives the temperature values and transmits them to the respective EG (EG_A), which forwards everything to EG_B. On the other side, *Network B* was composed by 26 nodes that monitor the relative humidity plus a sink connected to EG_B, which is responsible for averaging the values received after each measurement. Based on the data received from EG_A and on the stored averages, EG_B is able to set different WSN operation plans, and to communicate the required changes to its sink node in order to forward them to the wireless sensor nodes.

Adaptive Sensor Nodes Selection. We manually created three different sets of active nodes for the *Network B*: One with half of the nodes plus the sink; another with the other half plus the sink; and the last one with all nodes together. The first two plans are used for saving energy and are switched on every update to extend the WSN's lifetime, while the goal of the all-nodes plan is to provide more information about the environment. The downside is that this plan consumes more energy. Therefore, the latter is only used when the prediction produce *positive* outcomes and the environment is expected to change.

Adaptive Sampling. When the prediction outcome is a *positive* and changes are expected in *Network B*, nodes take measurements and transmit them every 30 seconds, consuming more energy and producing more information about the environment. Otherwise, this is done every 180 seconds.

4.1   Constant Predictions

At runtime, *Network B* defines how its nodes will react to environmental changes based on the predictions done: reporting more information when the environment is supposed to undergo variations and saving energy otherwise. In order to predict these variations, we calculated the average of the temperature and relative humidity values, without mixing data types, in discrete and sequential 5-minute window intervals. The absolute difference between the averages of two consecutive intervals is denoted Δ. In order to identify the data types, we used subscripts: Δ_T for temperature values and Δ_{RH} for relative humidity values. We have assumed that a large difference between the averages represent significant changes in the environment. Therefore, the system goal is to predict whether the next Δ will be over a determined threshold, τ, or not. To achieve that, we used a constant naïve model to make the predictions, i.e., in case of $\Delta > \tau$, we label it as *highΔ*, representing a *positive* outcome; otherwise, we call it a *lowΔ*.

In some cases, it may be useful to know if a *highΔ* means that the average is increasing or decreasing. In order to identify it, we added an additional notation to Δ. If the most recent average computed differs more than τ and is greater than the penultimate one, we mark it as *highΔ^+*; if it differs more than τ but is lower, we use *highΔ^-*, as shown in Figure 2. In case of having a *lowΔ*, there is no need for highlighting if the value is greater or less than the penultimate one.

Predictions are independent for each metric. Furthermore, any prediction is composed by three factors: the last two symptoms and the last prediction. The general idea is to try to learn the trend and avoid wrong predictions provoked by

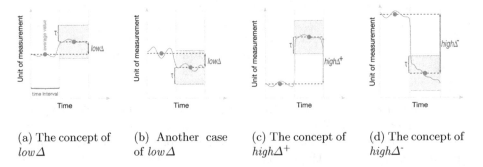

(a) The concept of *lowΔ*

(b) Another case of *lowΔ*

(c) The concept of *highΔ^+*

(d) The concept of *highΔ^-*

Fig. 2. How the system labels the Δs

Table 2. How the system reacts to the symptoms

Last Symptoms		Last Prediction	Prediction
$low\Delta$	$low\Delta$	any	$low\Delta$
$high\Delta^+$	$high\Delta^+$	any	$high\Delta^+$
$high\Delta^-$	$high\Delta^-$	any	$high\Delta^-$
$high\Delta^+$	any	$high\Delta^+$	$high\Delta^+$
$high\Delta^-$	any	$high\Delta^-$	$high\Delta^-$
$low\Delta$	any	$low\Delta$	$low\Delta$
$high\Delta^+$	$high\Delta^-$	$low\Delta$	$low\Delta$
$high\Delta^+$	$low\Delta$	$high\Delta^-$	$low\Delta$
$high\Delta^-$	$low\Delta$	$high\Delta^+$	$low\Delta$

noise and outliers. Thus, every time that two factors agree in one direction, the prediction is that, in the next interval, the environment will follow it. Otherwise, if the three factors are different, the prediction is that the environment will not undergo variations in the near future. Table 2 shows how we did the predictions using Δs.

Finally, if a *EG* receives information from internal and external sources, each prediction may be based on a different data type. In this case, it combines them in the simplest way: if one of the predictions is labeled as $high\Delta$, the final prediction is a $high\Delta$; otherwise, it is a $low\Delta$.

Adaptive Threshold. The value of τ is set based on the proportion of Δs seen in the historical data. For example, if the goal is to predict the highest quarter of Δs in a day, the threshold will be set at the 75th percentile of Δs. In this case, we identify it with the number 75 subscripted: τ_{75}.

Symptoms. To make those predictions, we must observe the measurements and find symptoms. A symptom, σ, is defined as a value where a $\Delta > \sigma$ represents a high probability of having $\Delta > \tau$ in the next interval. Therefore, if we notice that the most recent Δ is greater than σ, we have a symptom of $high\Delta$; otherwise, it is a symptom of $low\Delta$. Even though the concepts of σ and τ are similar, the numerical values may be different. For example, after observing the historical data, we might notice that every $\Delta > \tau_{40}$ calculated at time t was followed by a $\Delta > \tau_{75}$ at time $t + 1$. So, we would set the value of σ at the 40th percentile of Δs.

5   Evaluation

We considered each measurement done by the real nodes as the average of the network measurements in our simulations. Moreover, each set of measurements done by a node in a day was considered one day's worth of data. Therefore, we had enough data to simulate 48 different days. To check the feasibility of using this solution in the presented scenario, we evaluated the energy consumption in OMNeT++ [8] and the calculations about the performance score in Matlab. First, using OMNeT++ and MiXiM [9], we simulated the energy consumption based on TelosB nodes [10] using BMAC [11] as MAC protocol and a flooding routing protocol. In these simulations, the sensor nodes received new plans from the EG every 5 minutes, as explained in Section 3.2. We calculated the average energy consumption on each plan, considering also the energy spent to disseminate the plan changes through the network.

In Matlab, the data from the sensors were split into a training and a validation datasets to avoid overfitting. Each of these datasets was defined by a set of 24 days that were randomly selected on each run (repeated random sub-sampling validation). The model was fit to the training data, and predictive accuracy was assessed using the validation data. The tests were done over 10 different combinations of days and the final results were averaged over the splits. In the end, we checked how the system behaved when the plan of *Network B* was selected using only internal information (relative humidity values), only external information (temperature values) and combining both, and used the energy consumption levels to plot the results.

5.1   Training Dataset

After selecting 24 days for the training dataset, the measured values were used to set three different parameters:

- **The value of** τ – The threshold that the EGs must set. It was calculated as explained in 4.1, based on the measurements done during the training days.
- **The values of** σ**s** – The system built a table with the values of p based on percentiles, as shown in Figure 3d. The numerical value of σ_T and σ_{RH} was the same as the percentiles of Δ_T and Δ_{RH} with the highest value of p.

We assumed that the saved energy and the accuracy of the system have similar importance and set the value of $\alpha = 0.5$ in Equation 3. Figure 3a shows how much energy can be saved based on the thresholds that are used as symptoms of future changes. For example, at the point $(40, 20)$, any Δ_{RH} over the 40th percentile (i.e., greater than 40% of the values) is considered as a symptom of change, as well as any Δ_T over the 20th percentile. When a symptom is detected, the EG may launch a plan to produce more measurements in the next time-interval and, consequently, consume more energy. Figure 3b shows the total accuracy of the predictions and Figure 3c shows how the accuracy of *high*Δs changes depending on the threshold chosen to represent a symptom of changes in the future.

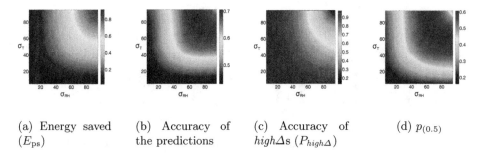

(a) Energy saved (E_{ps})

(b) Accuracy of the predictions

(c) Accuracy of $high\Delta s$ $(P_{high\Delta})$

(d) $p_{(0.5)}$

Fig. 3. Parameters obtained using the training data

5.2 Validating Dataset

The other 24 days were considered part of the validating dataset and their data were used to validate whether the system had chosen well and whether our hypothesis was valid. For this, the system used all the parameters calculated in the last step to calculate p.

5.3 Results

The plots in Figure 4 show the obtained results, where it is possible to see how much our solution was able to exploit the trade-off between the energy consumption and the quality of the measurements. To show better its benefits, we included two baseline scenarios that did not use collaboration: the first one saved the maximum energy possible by transmitting less measurements; the second did not save energy and always used the plan that transmits more measurements. An important remark is that both scenarios have $p_{(\alpha)} = 0$ for any α, because either they did not save any energy (the highest consumption plan case) or their accuracy of detecting $high\Delta s$ was zero (the lowest consumption plan case).

The results are split into three groups, according to the τ set for each case (τ_{70}, τ_{60} and τ_{50}). Each bar represents an average for the 24 days of the validation dataset. Observing the data, we can see that the correlation between temperature and relative humidity values is closer to -1 when we consider only the highest Δs, i.e., τ_{70}. Therefore, we assume that there are other factors that may influence the small variations in the relative humidity, such as the presence of persons close to the sensors. This explains why the percentage of $high\Delta s$ correctly predicted is lower when the system tries to track a higher number of changes (τ_{50}).

In Figures 4a and 4b, we can observe that, when we used only the plan that changed the number of active nodes, the system spent around 54% of the energy compared to the scenario in which the network was always producing more measurements. Also, Figure 4c shows that predictions can successfully improve the WSNs' operation. It is possible to see that, using only the relative humidity values as a reference (absence of external collaboration), 42.3% of the 5-minute intervals with $high\Delta_{RH}s$ were correctly predicted with τ_{60}. Compared to that, we can observe that the energy consumption increased much less than

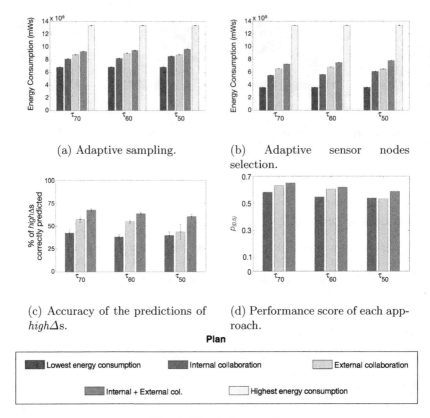

(a) Adaptive sampling.

(b) Adaptive sensor nodes selection.

(c) Accuracy of the predictions of $high\Delta$s.

(d) Performance score of each approach.

Fig. 4. Simulation results

the accuracy levels. For example, with τ_{60}, using the combination of internal and external information, the system was able to correctly predict 67.9% more $high\Delta$s consuming only 33.5% more energy. This means that the energy was used more intelligently in the second case.

Figure 4d shows that our approach for inter-WSN information exchange outperforms the other types of collaboration that use less information and spend their energy less efficiently. In summary, the trade-off between energy consumption and QoM was achieved and found to produce more effective results than the other approaches.

6   Conclusion and Future Work

Based on the presented results, it is possible to determine that our mechanism is able to use internal and external information to optimize the WSNs' performance, which is illustrated by the difference in the values of p. During the tests, we have also noticed that these improvements could be achieved only with data that is not only highly correlated, but there must also be a relation of causation between them. In this case, we noticed that changes in temperature led to changes in relative humidity, but the opposite was not necessarily true. Therefore, it would be more complex to make good predictions if we tried to predict temperature changes based on relative humidity values.

Although we made use of real data from existing experiments, we did generic calculations and assumptions that can be extended to numerous scenarios, in order to prove the general idea of this concept. We expect that specific knowledge about different scenarios may lead to better results. For example, as shown in [12], when the relative humidity is over 50%, it is possible to calculate its value based on information about the temperature only. Thus, in a scenario similar to ours, the system could save even more energy by letting the EG calculate the local data based on external information.

The next steps include adapt this solution to an autonomic system, as described in [2]. That is, a more generic mechanism which is able to work with other WSN types and is able to work with other prediction methods that may have better performance in different scenarios. Additionally, the idea of an autonomic solution involves a pro-active and self-managing system, which improves the information fusion and the decision optimization, besides creating specific plans for the WSNs according to the predictions about the near future.

Acknowledgement. This work has been partially supported by the Spanish Government through the project TEC2012-32354 (Plan Nacional I+D), by the Catalan Government through the project SGR2009#00617 and by the European Union through the project FP7-SME-2013-605073-ENTOMATIC.

References

1. Pal, S., Oechsner, S., Bellalta, B., Oliver, M.: Performance optimization of multiple interconnected heterogeneous sensor networks via collaborative information sharing. Journal of Ambient Intelligence and Smart Environments **5**(4), 403–413 (2013)
2. Dias, G.M.: Performance optimization of wsns using external information. In: 2013 IEEE 14th International Symposium and Workshops on a World of Wireless, Mobile and Multimedia Networks (WoWMoM), pp. 1–2 (2013)
3. Dressler, F., Awad, A., Gerla, M.: Inter-domain routing and data replication in virtual coordinate based networks. In: 2010 IEEE International Conference on Communications, pp. 1–5. IEEE, May 2010
4. Parker, L.E.: Detecting and monitoring time-related abnormal events using a wireless sensor network and mobile robot. In: 2008 IEEE/RSJ International Conference on Intelligent Robots and Systems, pp. 3292–3298. IEEE, September 2008
5. Yann-Ael, L.B., Bontempi, G.: Round robin cycle for predictions in wireless sensor networks. In: 2005 International Conference on Intelligent Sensors, Sensor Networks and Information Processing, pp. 253–258. IEEE (2005)
6. Deshpande, A., Guestrin, C., Madden, S.R., Hellerstein, J.M., Hong, W.: Model-driven data acquisition in sensor networks. In: Proceedings of the Thirtieth International Conference on Very Large Data Bases, vol. 30, pp. 588–599 (2004)
7. Oechsner, S., Bellalta, B., Dimitrova, D., Hossfeld, T.: Visions and challenges for sensor network collaboration in the cloud. In: The Seventh International Conference on Innovative Mobile and Internet Services in Ubiquitous Computing (2014)

8. Varga, A.: The OMNeT++ discrete event simulation system. In: Proceedings of the European Simulation Multiconference (ESM 2001), vol. 9 (2001)
9. Köpke, A., Swigulski, M., Wessel, K., Willkomm, D., Parker, T.E.V., Kleinhaneveld, P.T., Visser, O.W, Lichte, H.S., Valentin, S.: Simulating Wireless and Mobile Networks in OMNeT ++ The MiXiM Vision
10. Inc., Crossbow Technology. TelosB Mote Platform. Rev B
11. Fakih, K., Diouris, J.-F., Andrieux, G.: BMAC: beamformed MAC protocol with channel tracker in MANET using smart antennas. In: 2006 European Conference on Wireless Technologies, vol. 2, pp. 185–188. IEEE, September 2006
12. Lawrence, M.G.: The Relationship between Relative Humidity and the Dewpoint Temperature in Moist Air: A Simple Conversion and Applications. Bulletin of the American Meteorological Society **86**(2), 225–233 (2005)

A Study of Energy Efficiency Techniques Using DRX for Handover Management in LTE-A Networks

Tanu Goyal[✉] and Sakshi Kaushal[✉]

Computer Science and Engineerig, UIET, Panjab University, Chandigarh, India
tanugoyal27@gmail.com, sakshi@pu.ac.in

Abstract. For Internet access, smart phones and tablets have started replacing traditional computers. This change got encouraged with technological development like high-resolution screens, powerful processes and compact, long-lasting batteries. With numerous wireless technologies like Global Positioning System (GPS), Cellular and Wi-Fi etc., the mobile device is always connected to network and ready to perform tasks using various applications. The video conferencing and background application like messaging need higher throughput and need to be on network always, which results into regular battery consumption. So, with the recent increase of mobile data usage and the emergence of new applications, such as multimedia online gaming, mobile TV, Web 2.0, and streaming contents, have motivated the development of Long Term Evolution (LTE) and Long Term Evolution (LTE)-Advanced (A) technologies. In LTE, Discontinuous Reception (DRX) feature focused on the objective to make User Equipment (UE) energy efficient by saving battery. In this paper, we have explored and analyzed various methods in which DRX technique is used in LTE-A. We have also attempted to identify the role and impact of DRX on handover in LTE-A along with some directions future work.

Keywords: LTE-A · Handover · DRX · Power saving · Delay · Multimedia

1 Introduction

The latest discovery in networking has developed a new trend in the mobile market. This mobile market has created a new variety of smart devices, e.g., smart phones, tablets, windows etc. and replacing traditional computers. This changes got encouraged with technological development like high resolution screens, powerful processes and compact long lasting batteries with numerous wireless technology like GPS, cellular communication, Wi-Fi etc. The mobile device is always connected to the network and ready to perform tasks using various applications for multimedia traffics like video streaming, video conferencing and background applications like messaging need higher throughput and need to always on network always. The Third Generation (3G) does not have ability to provide services

© Springer International Publishing Switzerland 2015
M. Jonsson et al. (Eds.): MACOM 2015, LNCS 9305, pp. 33–44, 2015.
DOI: 10.1007/978-3-319-23440-3_3

to multimedia traffics because it has low transmission rate, high latency and high in cost. In the mobile communication system multimedia services and broadband services are strongly demanding with higher data rate, bandwidth, fast accessibility and connectivity everywhere. For this, IMT-Advanced has proposed a next-generation mobile communication system called as Fourth Generation (4G) [1]. Third Generation Partnership Project (3GPP) presented the Long Term Evolution (LTE)-Advanced (A) Release 10 (R10) to Internet Telecommunication Unit (ITU); meet the need of 4G. LTE-A meets the requirement of high speed [2]. LTE-A provides upto 1Gbps in Downlink (DL) and 500 Mbps in Uplink (UL). With the help of LTE-A users can use high speed service anywhere.

4G has capability to provide services to various smart phones or devices. But the reliability, seamless connectivity, etc., depends on handover performance. For providing Quality of Service (QoS) handover is a key element. The main issue in LTE-A is battery life. In LTE-A, Discontinuous Reception (DRX) feature focus on the objective to make UE energy efficient by saving battery. As number of multimedia service increases and life of battery degrades. This problem of drainage is even more accelerated day by day. DRX is used to save the battery power by switching off RF circuitry whenever there is no packets in the network. In this paper, we have explored various methods in which DRX technique has been used in LTE-A. We have also attempted to identify the role and impact of DRX on handover in LTE-A by presenting and analyzing various techniques and mechanisms proposed.

The rest of the paper is organized as follows: Section 2 introduces the handover, different type of handover and phases of handover. Section 3 describes the issues related to LTE-A and their proposed solutions. Section 4 describes the effect of DRX with handover and some directions for future research work. Section 5 concludes the paper.

2   Handover

Handover is the process transferring one ongoing call from one cell to another cell without loss of packets. Another reason of using handover, when the capacity of the one cell is almost full and to provide connectivity to ongoing call, call connects to another cell. In other words, handover provides un-interrupted connections of mobile device with its gateway and ensures better Quality of Service (QoS) in the network bib3. But the main issue during handover is of power consumption. As the user moves from one cell to another the mobile battery gets consumed.

2.1   Types of Handover in LTE

This section describes the various types of handover:

• **Hard Handover:** It is also known as break before make?, as there is a short disconnection in order to achieve the conversion of carrier frequency. It is manly occurs in the Time Division Multiple Access (TDMA) and Frequency Division

Multiple Access (FDMA). LTE and LTE-A mainly use hard handover which results in high latency, unreliable in nature, high outage probability and high data loss bib2.

• **Soft Handover:** It is also known as make before break?. A new wireless link to the target eNodeB is established while the old connection with source eNodeB is maintained.

• **Softer Handover:** In this, one cell is divided into a number of sectors. Handover takes place between the sectors within the same cell or between the sectors of different cells.

• **Relay Handover:** It is basically used in the Time Division-Synchronous Code Division Multiple Access (TD-SCDMA), it is based on the smart antenna technology. Relay handover can take place between the cells that are using different frequencies bib4.

• **Vertical Handover** (Inter Handover): This type of handover is occurs between different wireless technologies such as handover from LTE network to the WiMAX.

• **Horizontal Handover** (Intra Handover): Handover takes places in the same wireless technology, e.g., handover of User Equipment (UE) from cell to other cell such as in LTE system.

2.2   Phases of Handover

In this section, various phases of handover is described [5,6]

1. Initiation: The MS measures the channel quality such as Received Signal Strength (RSS), Signal to Interference Ratio (SIR), distance , etc., This is also known as handover measurement. Handover measurement is the combination of the measurement control and Measurement Report (MR). MR contains the resource availability and the network load.

2. Network selection: As the report gets generated in initiation phase, the best eNodeB is selected to maintain the connection. The handover decision is made in this step.

3. Execution: UE starts to set up a connection with the target eNodeB.

3   Main Issue of LTE-A

In LTE-A, data rate can be increased by using carrier aggregation, high modulation techniques, advanced coding techniques and advanced multi-antenna techniques etc. but due to complex mechanism, battery of UE get degrade. Battery consumption of UE is the main issue of LTE-A. Video streaming, video conferencing and background applications like messaging need higher throughput and need UE to always be on network. This causes the battery consumption problem. There are two states in LTE-A RRC_ Connected state and RRC_ Idle state. RRC_ Connected state is also known as active state, UE remains in RRC_ Connected state whenever there is packet to receive/transmit. RRC_ Idle state is also known as inactive state, it mean UE does not have traffic to receive/transmit but the UE will remain registered with the network and it had unique identifier along with it. Whenever there is packet in the network, the eNodeB sends the request of connection, UE immediately comes into RRC_ Connected mode. But the applications like facebook, twitter are sending very small packets in background so, the UE cannot remain in idle mode. This causes battery degradation problem. Sometimes status update messages are also passing through and this causes the unrestrained signals.

When there is packet coming from higher layer, the UE goes into the connected state. The main point is to consider here; if there is no packet to send/receive, the UE will have to stay in the connected state until the Inactivity Timer gets expire. This is the additional time that UE has to spend in active state. This additional time is named as a Tail Time (TT) [7,8]. To overcome the issue of TT, 3G worked on new technology named as Fast Dormancy (FD). FD allows the UE to go back into idle mode, when there is no packet in the network without waiting for the expiration time and by releasing the signal [8]. But this technique also causes a problem of overloading of signals such as connection and disconnection signals [9]. LTE-A introduces the DRX/DTX for saving the battery life.

3.1 DRX/DTX

DRX concept is not new, it is also used in Second Generation (2G) and 3G. LTE-A uses the feature of DRX for saving power of UE. DRX/DTX is able to increase the battery life through monitoring the activity of UE [10]. In Universal Mobile Terrestrial System (UMTS), DRX uses three parameters like wakeup, sleep and Inactivity Timer. The main focus of using DRX is to improve battery consumption. In LTE-A, Light Sleep (Ls) and Deep sleep (Ds) concept are used for more improvement in the power consumption. In Ls mode, UE stays in sleep for shorter period of time and does not come into idle mode properly and consumes less power as compare to active mode. In this mode, UE comes frequently sleep to active mode to receive packets. In case of Ds mode, UE stays in sleep mode for longer period of time. The consumption of energy is almost negligible. But this power saving method is also affect the QoS as delay of packet increases.

3.2 DRX Steps

The following describes the stages of UE during DRX cycle, On-duration, Inactivity Timer, Sleep state [11].

• **DRX cycle:** It provides the difference in time between the starting of two consecutive On-duration intervals in which the UE remains active. The cycle consist of On-duration followed by sleep interval. But the length of the DRX cycle affects the QoS. If the length of DRX cycle is long, than delay increases accordingly and vice versa.

• **On-duration (tod):** It is the time when UE is in active state and listen to the

Physical Downlink Control Channel (PDCCH). If there is any data scheduled for UE, Inactivity Timer get started otherwise UE goes back to sleep mode, it might be Ds or Ls.

- **Inactivity Timer:** During tod time, if there is any packet listened at DL than, Inactivity Timer get starts and receives data packets. During this, in case there is another packet arrives, the Inactivity Timer get starts from starting to receive more packets. When Inactivity Timer expires, the UE goes back to sleep mode.
- **Sleep Mode:** It consist of two sleep modes i.e. Ls and Ds. In Ls mode, UE stays in sleep for shorter period of time and does not come into idle mode properly and consumes less power as compare to active mode. In this mode, UE comes frequently from sleep to active mode to receive packets. In case of Ds mode, UE stays in sleep mode for longer period of time. The consumption of energy is almost negligible.

According to Fig. 1, it shows the typical scenario of DRX operation.

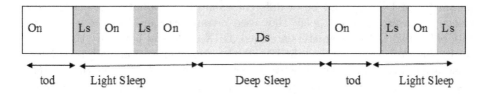

Fig. 1. A typical Scenario of DRX operation

When there is no traffic to receive/ transmit for long period of time, UE releases its connection and eNodeB removes the UE from its Database (DB). This is the ideal mode of DRX. In this mode, UE periodically listen to the PDCCH in DL to check any packets and follows the DRX cycle. In case of idle mode, network does not know the existence of UE. UE checks the signal strength. According to the signal strength, the new serving eNodeB is selected. The new serving eNodeB announces the system information without its tracking area. Then UE announces its tracking area and shows its presence in the network. So, that network can page the UE when there is packet to send.

When there is packet in the DL, UE pages with the network and enter into the connected mode. There might be delay. This delay depends on the time taken to page within the network, to enter into the connected mode and time taken for synchronization with UL. For reduction of delay, the paging DRX cycle should be optimized.

In the sleep mode, there is higher latency because rate of packet drop increases. In [12] authors explained that throughput is the another issue while using DRX. They explained throughput of the system, depends on the channel condition. Authors presented the adaptive DRX inactivity timer for improvement of throughput. If the channel quality is bad, the UE goes back into the sleep mode for small amount of time and the transmission time increases. In [13] author presented the effect of DRX functionality on LTE-A and found out that with higher power saving, packet loss increases and vice versa. In [14] DRX parameters had been checked out the balance between the power saving and the throughput of a single user.

Ali *et. al.* [15] had taken the case of active and background traffic and developed the analytical model for power saving and delay. Through the DRX, configuration performance parameter was derived and found out the tradeoff between the power saving and latency. They showed that with the application, latency requirement changes. For adaption of DRX setting, DRX configuration switching mechanism had been discussed based upon the changing in application running. They adapted the DRX parameters according the traffic ongoing and this method improved the power saving and delay latency.

Scott *et. al.* [16] compared the fixed sized frame DRX cycle to adjustable frame DRX cycle by using semi-Markov process. The analytical results showed that fixed sized frame DRX cycle behaves differently than adjustable frame DRX cycle. In [17,18] worked on the UMTS and took Poisson arrival process and ETSI busty traffic model [19] and described that for handling the varying traffic the parameter of DRX should be of different value. For evaluation of energy efficiency and average packet delay, they used Z-transform and Laplace transform. In UMTS, two DRX parameters are used, DRX cycle and inactivity time.

In [20] the authors checked the UE activity autonomously and adjusted DRX cycle accordingly for balance between power saving and delay in the packets instead of switching between the short and long DRX cycle. In [21] authors extended the time of nth DRX short cycle by doubling the time of (n-1)th DRX short cycle. In [22] authors used divide-and-conquer method for active and sleep operations. They described the power saving factor and average packet transmission delay by analyzing the expected time of each mode.

In [23] authors used the semi-Markov model to find out the probability of UE to stay in each state and its transmission probability in different states. They had taken three states. One is active period, Ds period and Ls period. By checking the transmission probability the expected delay was calculated by multiplying the probability of occurrence of each individual state. In [24,25] authors worked on the probability theory for analysis of power saving and delay. They had not taken much parameter due to limitation of space. They showed only preliminary results for correctness and feasibility. Chih *et. al.* [26] showed that DRX is best technique for reduction of power consumption and delay. These two parameters are contradictory to each other. They used recursive deduction and Markov model for in-depth analysis of power saving and delay. They used the mixed DRX short and long cycle. For arrival of packets, they had taken the Poisson packet arrival. They observed the network by using short and long cycle and analysis that, the proper choice of parameter can save power and reduce delay.

3.3   Use of DRX in Various Applications

Voice over Internet Protocol (VoIP): VoIP is bi-directional in nature and for applying DRX is not feasible as such. In VoIP, the packets will be pass in the periodic manner. In LTE-A, when there is no packet in the network to receive/transmit, UE goes back into DRX cycle for Ls and wake up immediately to senses the PDCCH in DL of the network.

Video streaming: In the video streaming, the frames will be received in the fixed or constant rate. In the frames, the packets will be of fixed or varying sizes [27]. In video streaming, if the speed of the data frames is less, than it causes delay. Delay is the main issue in real time applications. But in case of DRX, If Ls is applying and the speed of data increases, than it would not affect the streaming of packets. Packets can send/receive in high speed and delay could not occur. The best method for applying DRX in video streaming is exponentially increases the DRX cycle from Ls to Ds.

In [14] studied the DRX parameter on the basis of power saving and its impact on the QoS of VoIP by using dynamic and semi persistent packet scheduling. The author found out that, the power saving is high for the semi persistent scheduling, than the dynamic packet scheduling by using lower spectral efficiency.

Zhou *et. al.* [28] used the semi-Markov model for the purpose of power saving in LTE networks. This showed that in active state UE consume 0.5 W/TTI. But in case of Ls it consume only 0.011 W/TTI. This showed that the power saving is approximately 0.489 W/TTI. Whenever UE entered into Ds, it did not consume any power. This showed that UE remained fully power saver mode in Ds.

Ramli *et. al.* [29] they worked on the assignment of resources and indicate that Best Channel Quality Indicator (BCQI) assigned the channel to only those UEs that had best channel condition. It did not assign channel to those UE that does not had good quality channel. This channel quality is calculated through the Channel Quality Indicator (CQI).

Lin. *et. al.* [30] they used the Channel-Adapted and Buffer-Aware (CACB) scheme that was used for the scheduling of packets. This scheme was basically used for the QoS related to real time system. This was used to check the buffer length, CQI, separated the real time and non-real time traffic.

Delgado *et. al.* [31] packet scheduling and admission control scheme was used. They used the time domain schedule and frequency domain schedule. This maximized the throughput of the network and the delay of the network reduced and did not cross the threshold value. This algorithm was used in real time and non-real time applications.

4   Effect of DRX on Handover Decision

When LTE is in DRX sleep mode; the UE can switched off its activity for some predetermine time period. It saves the battery life and the authors showed that this method provide high latency [32]. In this two methods are proposed for the efficiency of DRX operation based upon the handover. One method is of continuous monitoring and other is shorter DRX period on the predetermine time. The predetermine time is determined by the eNodeB and it cannot be determine by the UE accurately. In [33,35] they had worked on DRX by using adjusting DRX parameters and found out tradeoff between the latency and power saving. In [36], authors considered the DRX for the power saving in case of handover. In [37], it is related to the communication device that have a feature of handover with DRX operations. In this paper, handover was done in connected mode along with the DRX operations. When there is cell change, UE sends cell change report to the serving-eNodeB and resume the operation of DRX. Serving-eNodeB remained in waiting state until it receive the DRX resume command along with the command message from the target-eNodeB. When resumed command is received along with command message, the DRX operations transmitted from active to sleep mode. This operations helps in reduction of battery life when handover occurs.

In [38] researcher proposed a new technique named as Longest Awake Time (LAT) for improvement of latency and power saving. In it, UE gradually increase the tod time from initial value when the handover decision is made by the eNodeB. When UE received the handover command message serving eNodeB notify the UE to stop increasing the tod gradually. If LAT is not used, the network face additional delay. The following steps takes place during initialization of handover [38]:

1. UE measures the signal strength from the serving-eNodeB and closest-eNodeB. For this if the following condition met UE send the MR to serving-eNodeB.

$$Rn + oftn + octn > Rs + ofsn + ocsn + offp + hysp$$

2. serving-eNodeB uses the received MR from UE and request for handover to target-eNodeB. The UE stops sending MR until the following condition is met.

$$Rn + oftn + octn < Rs + ofsn + ocsn + offp - hysp$$

where Rs and Rn are Reference Signal Received Power (RSRP) and Reference Signal Received Quality (RSRQ), hysp is hysteresis parameter for MR. offp hysteresis parameter for handover this prevent the mobile from moving back to original cells. ofsn, oftn these are the offset for serving-eNodeB and target-eNodeB for finding optional frequency. Ocsn, ocnn offset for the serving- eNodeB and target-eNodeB for findng optional cell specific. The following algorithms has been used for the operations of UE side during LAT and the LAT operation on serving- eNodeB, respectively.

LAT improves the performance and it saves the battery life. With the help of LAT, the sleep period becomes shorter, when handover decision is made by serving-eNodeB, UE increases the on-duration timer gradually, so that, DRX cycle cannot change. Algorithm 1 and 2 shows, the stage of LAT in UE side and serving-eNodeB side. This work basically focused on intra-handover; the inter-

---

Algorithm 1. UE side during LAT [38]

Begin:

1: UE sends MR to serving-eNodeB and checks if handover condition is satisfied.
2: UE waits until Acknowledgment (Ack) from serving-eNodeB.
3: if ACK received then serving-eNodeB sends LAT notification to UE and ask to increase tod gradually. Goto Step 5.
4: else Resume DRX operations and wait for MR.
5: if target- eNodeB grants resources for handover.
6: Handover request Ack msessage (msg) sends serving-eNodeB.
7: serving-eNodeB forward command message to UE.
8: if UE is Awake command message is send directly and serving-eNodeB inform UE to stop tod increasing gradually.
9: else message will be buffered at serving-eNodeB and wait until next DRX awake.
10: once UE receives handover command.
11: handover preparation procedure is completed and handover execution phase will be perform.
12: Exit.

Algorithm 2. Serving-eNodes during LAT [38]

Begin:

1: Handover is triggered.
2: serving- eNodeB receivesMR from UE.
3: if handover is made, serving-eNodeB sends LAT message to UE and ask UE to increased tod gradually.
4: else wait for MR
5: serving-eNodeB request message to the target-eNodeB and waits for handover Ack message.
6: serving-eNodeB sends command message to UE
7: if UE is Awake, command message is send directly and serving-eNodeB inform UE to stop tod increasing gradually.
8: else message will be buffered at serving-eNodeB and wait until next DRX awake.
9: if handover command message is send immediately to UE.
10: Delay $= 0$ also modified UE to stop tod gradually increasing.
11: if LAT= Awake, power consumed.
12: else, power $=$ saved
13: Exit.

---

handover and other features like inactivity timer, sleep time all these can also be considered in future.

According to extensive literature review, DRX mechanism is widely adopted in LTE to conserve the mobile phone's battery resources and saving over-the-air resource on both the uplink and downlink to increase overall system capacity. But this mechanism results in higher handover latency due to its sleep period which affects performance of applications like video-streaming, etc. In order to minimize the handover latency, there is a need to optimize the DRX parameters dynamically also. To achieve a seamless mobility across radio cells, LTE implements handover procedures. Service degradation is experienced due to frequent handovers in LTE network with introduction of small cells to improve LTE coverage (intra-LTE handovers) and Inter-Radio Access Technology (IRAT) handovers to legacy GSM/UMTS networks. Handover latency also sometimes contributes to the poor performance of the delay-sensitive applications in LTE.

Since there has not been significant work on the above two issues together, hence the study of impact of DRX on real-time applications such as video-streaming combined with handover performance in optimized manner is still an area which needs to be focused and which would yield productivity as well as performance for both network and user.

5   Conclusion

Various Internet applications, like video conferencing, different background application, i.e, messaging, etc., need higher throughput and need to be on network always which results into regular battery consumption. In this paper, we have explored various methods in which DRX technique is used in LTE. We have also attempted to identify the role and impact of DRX on handover in LTE. We described the detailed description of DRX during handover and presented various ways of using DRX parameters in handover to overcome the battery drainage problem. One of the methods is Longer Awake Time. This helps to reduce drainage of battery life by removing DRX sleep period. In future, dynamic energy efficient mechanism needs to be devised that will improve battery life of user equipment and would also reduce signaling load through optimized handover procedure leading to improvement in service performance.

References

1. Guangxiang, Y., Zhang, X., Wang, W., Yang, Y.: Carrier aggregation for LTE-advanced mobile communication systems. IEEE Communications Magazine **48**, 88–93 (2010)
2. chang, J., Technol, H., Li, Y., Feng, S., Wang, H.: A fractional soft handover scheme for 3GPP LTE- advanced system. In: IEEE International Conference on Communications Workshops, ICC Workshops, pp. 1–5 (2009)
3. Jihai, H., Bingyang, W.: Handover in the 3GPP long term evolution (LTE) systems. In: Mobile Congress, Global, pp. 1–6 (2010)
4. Bo, L., Dongliang, X., Shiduan, C., Junliang, C., Ping, Z., Zhu, W., Bin, L.: Recent advances on TD-SCDMA in china. IEEE Communication Magazine **43**, 30–37 (2005)
5. Sgora, A., Vergados, D.D.: Handoff prioritization and decision schemes in wireless cellular networks: a survey. IEEE Communication Survey Tutorial **11**, 57–77 (2009)
6. 3rd Generation Partnership Project, Technical Specification Group Radio Access Network, Evolved Universal Terrestrial Radio Access (E-UTRA) and Evolved Terrestrial Radio Access Network (E-UTRAN), overall description, stage 2 (release 11), 3GPP TS 36.300, vol. 11.4.0 (2013)
7. Bontu, C., Illidge, E.: DRX mechanism for power saving in LTE. IEEE Communication Magazine **47**(6), 48–55 (2009)

8. LTE RAN Enhancement for Diverse Data Applications. 3GPP TR 36.822, vol. 11 (2012)
9. Evolved Universal Terrestrial Radio Access (E-UTRA); Radio Resource Control (RRC); Protocol Specification. 3GPP TS 36.331, Rel. 9, vol. 12 (2012)
10. 3GPP TS 36.300 V12.0.0. Evolved Universal Terrestrial Radio Access (E-UTRA) and Evolved Universal Terrestrial Radio Access Network (E- UTRAN). Overall Description; Stage 2 (2013)
11. 3GPP. Evolved Universal Terrestrial Radio Access (E-UTRA), Radio Resource Control (RRC). In: Technical Specification, TS 36.331 version 11.0.0 Rel. 11 (2012)
12. Gao, S., Tian, H., Zhu, J., Chen, L.: A more power-efficient adaptive discontinuous reception mechanism in LTE. In: Proc. IEEE VTC- Fall, pp. 1–5 (2011)
13. Kolding, T., Wigard, J., Dalsgaard, L.: Balancing power saving and single user experience with discontinuous reception in LTE. In: Proc. IEEE Int. Symp. ISWCS, pp. 713–717 (2008)
14. Polignano, M., Vinella, D., Laselva, D., Wigard, J., Sorensens, T.: Power savings and QoS impact for VoIP application with DRXDTX feature in LTE. In: Proc. IEEE VTC, pp. 1–5. Spring (2011)
15. Koc, A.: Device power saving and latency optimization in LTE-A networks through DRX configuration, pp. 1–12 (2014)
16. Fowler, S., Bhamber, R.S., Mellouk, A.: Analysis of adjustable and fixed DRX mechanism for power saving in LTE/LTE-advanced. In: IEEE International Conference. IEEE (2012)
17. Yang, S.R., Lin, Y.B.: Modeling UMTS discontinuous reception mechanism. IEEE Transaction Wireless Communication 4(1), 312319 (2005)
18. Yang, S.R., Yan, S.Y., Hung, H.N.: Modeling UMTS power saving with bursty packet data traffic. IEEE Transaction Mob. Computer 6(12), 13981409 (2007)
19. ETSI Technical Report UMTS 30.03 version 3.2.0, Universal Mobile Telecommunications System (UMTS); Selection Procedures for the Choice of Radio Transmission Technologies of the UMTS (1998)
20. Liu, E., Zhang, J., Ren, W.: Adaptive and autonomous power-saving scheme for beyond 3G user equipment. IET Communications 7(7), 602610 (2013)
21. Fowler, S., Bhamber, S., Mellouk, A.: Analysis of adjustable and xed DRX mechanism for power saving in LTE/LTE-advanced. In: Proc. IEEE ICC, pp. 1964–1969 (2012)
22. Jin, S., Qiao, D.: Numerical analysis of the power saving in 3GPP LTE advanced wireless networks. IEEE Transaction Vehicular Technology 61, 1779–1785 (2012)
23. Mihov, Y.Y., Kassev, K.M., Tsankov, B.P.: Analysis and performance evaluation of the DRX mechanism for power saving in LTE. In: Proc. IEEE 26th Convention of Electrical and Electronics Engineers in Israel, pp. 520524 (2010)
24. Wang, H.C., Tseng, C.C., Chen, G.Y., Kuo, F.C., Ting, K.-C.: Accurate analysis of delay and power consumption of LTE DRX mechanism with a combination of short and long cycles. In: Proc. The 15th International Symposium on Wireless Personal Multimedia Communications (WPMC) (2012)
25. Wang, H.C., Tseng, C.C., Chen, G.Y., Kuo, F.-C., Ting, K.-C.: Power saving by LTE DRX mechanism using a mixture of short and long cycles. In: Proc. IEEE TENCON, Xian, China (2013)
26. Tseng, C.-C.: Delay and Power Consumption in LTE/LTE-A DRX Mechanism with Mixed Short and Long Cycles. IEEE Transactions on Vehicular Technology (2015)
27. 3GPP2 C.R.1002-0, CDMA2000 Evaluation Methodology (2004)

28. 3GPP. TSG RAN WG2, LTE contribution. In: Technical specication, TS 36.300, N. R2–071285 (2007)
29. Ramil, H.A.M., Basukala, R., Sandrasegaran, K., Patachaianand, R.: Performance of well-known packet scheduling algorithms in the downlink 3GPP LTE system. In: IEEE 9th Malaysia International Conference on Communications (MICC), pp. 815–20 (2009)
30. Yan, L., Guangxin, Y.: Channel-adapted and buffer-aware packet scheduling in LTE wireless communication system. In: 4th International Conference on Wireless Communications, Networking and Mobile Computing (WiCOM), pp. 1–4 (2008)
31. Delgado O, Jaumard, B.: Joint admission control and resource allocation with GoS and QoS in LTE uplink. In: IEEE GLOBECOM workshops (GC Wkshps), pp. 829–33 (2010)
32. Wu, W., Womack, J.E., Cai, Z.: Method and System for Efficient DRX Operation during Handover in LTE, US Patent 8,023,467 (2011)
33. Zhou, L., Xu, H., Tian, H., Gao, Y., Du, L., Chen, L.: Performance analysis of power saving mechanism with adjustable DRX cycles in 3GPP LTE. In: IEEE 68th Vehicular Technology Conference, pp. 1–5 (2008)
34. Mihov, Y., Kassev, K., Tsankov, B.: Analysis and performance evaluation of the DRX mechanism for power saving in LTE. In: Electrical and Electronics Engineers in Israel (IEEEI), pp. 000520–000524 (2010)
35. Koc, A.T., Jha, S.C., Vannithamby, R., Torlak, M.: Optimizing DRX configuration to improve battery power saving and latency of active mobile applications over LTE-A network. In: Wireless Communications and Networking Conference (WCNC), pp. 568–573 (2013)
36. Kim, S.-H., Van Lieshout, G.J., Jeong, K.-I., Van Der, V.H.: Handover of user equipment (UE) during discontinuous reception (DRX) operation in mobile communication system, EP Patent 1,915,010 (2011)
37. Kim, S.-H.: Suwon-Si, Gyeonggi-do (KR), Handover of user equipment (UE) during discontinuous reception (DRX) operation in mobile communication system, EP Patent 1915010A2 (2008)
38. Liu,Y.: Optimization of discontinuous reception (DRX) operation during intra-LTE handover. Global Information Infrastructure Symposium, operation in mobile communication system, EP Patent 1,915,010 (2011)

PHY

Sequential Incomplete Information Game in Relay Networks Based on Wireless Physical Layer Network Coding

Tomas Hynek$^{(\boxtimes)}$ and Jan Sykora

Faculty of Electrical Engineering, Czech Technical University in Prague,
Technicka 2, 166 27 Prague, Czech Republic
{hynektom,Jan.Sykora}@fel.cvut.cz

Abstract. A performance of a network based on Wireless Physical Layer Network Coding (WPLNC) crucially depends on local mapping functions selected by every individual relay. As a whole the mappings must enable the destination to recover desired source data but they must also be reasonable from relays' point of view. This is important especially in distributed and decentralised networks where the relays' mappings are not given in advance but they emerge from interaction among relays.

In this paper we focus on a toy example of relay network where a sequential selection of the WPLNC mappings takes place. We assume that the first relay may suffer from low battery level which may affect its selection of WPLNC mappings and that the second relay can deduce the battery state from observed actions and alter its behaviour to cope with the situation. For this scenario we discuss and evaluate an existence of game equilibria.

Keywords: Relay network · Wireless physical layer network coding · Sequential game · Perfect Bayesian Equilibrium

1 Introduction

Wireless physical layer network coding (WPLNC) was shown to be a way to improve performance (gain, reliability, energy efficiency, etc.) of multi-node communication networks [1]. WPLNC extends the ideas of network coding [2] to wireless communication networks. Individual transmissions are no longer forced to be separated in an orthogonal way, but they are allowed to overlap. Direct processing of superimposed signals is a source of competitive advantage of WPLNC over classical routing solution. The down side is the complicated and demanding signal processing at relays and destinations. Nevertheless with rapid progress in DSP technology the price to be paid is getting lower.

Various coding and signal processing techniques for WPLNC have been proposed in recent years. To mention a few of them: analogue processing based Amplify and Forward [3,4], lattice based Compute and Forward [5] and various forms of Decode and Forward schemes [3,6–8].

© Springer International Publishing Switzerland 2015
M. Jonsson et al. (Eds.): MACOM 2015, LNCS 9305, pp. 47–56, 2015.
DOI: 10.1007/978-3-319-23440-3_4

2   Motivation

The most of current research works assume centralised control of the relay network, where the relays are given their appropriate operation and are forced to beneficially cooperate to provide source to destination communication. Our interest is focused on decentralised networks where node operations are not given but rather arise from mutual node interactions. A sensor or an ad-hoc network is an example of such a distributed network.

Since the WPLNC is quite sensitive to the selection of mapping functions the maliciously behaving node may cause significant damage to the network simply by selecting improper WPLNC mapping. The malicious behaviour can be either intentional when evil node attacks the network or unintentional when the node running out of battery selects unexpected mappings to grab its last chance to deliver data.

The presence of intentionally malicious behaving node among the fair players is widely analysed in the area of sensor networks. Game theoretical approach to coexistence in point to point scenario is presented in [9]. Relay networks (with single or multiple relay) with malicious nodes are in [10,11] however both are single source cases. Our focus in this paper is mostly laid on unintentional malicious behaviour caused by emptying battery that forces the relay to be selfish and use the most energy saving WPLNC mappings.

It is also important to note that since we are focused on sensor networks, where the node are mostly simple battery powered devices that are not capable of any advanced channel coding technique, we investigate uncoded communication.

3   System Model

A network of interest consists of two independent sources S_1, S_2, two relays $\mathcal{R}_R, \mathcal{R}_C$, where subscript R stands for row and C for column to distinguish the game players, and a destinations $\mathcal{D}$, see Fig.1. This is a multi-relay and wireless extension of the well-known butterfly network [2]. It is also the simplest network that can illustrate the issues studied here. The networks with more nodes are obviously possible but their analysis is impractical, however, the results shown in this paper can be straightforwardly extended.

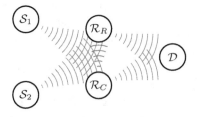

Fig. 1. Two relay network with $\mathcal{R}_C$ to $\mathcal{R}_R$ signalling

The important aspect of this paper is that we assume that the relay $\mathcal{R}_C$ can suffer from low battery situation with probability p. When it is depleting its resources its main intent is to deliver as much as possible information to the destination in the most energy saving way. The other relay $\mathcal{R}_R$ has available observation of $\mathcal{R}_C$'s actions (shown in red in Fig.1) and can deduce his battery state and consequently support it. Since the $\mathcal{R}_C$ knows about its battery state we will call it an informed relay (player). The uninformed one – $\mathcal{R}_R$ – has only a chance to learn about $\mathcal{R}_C$ state from the received signal.

Note that the transmissions of the source nodes are not orthogonally separated i.e. relay $\mathcal{R}_i$, $i \in \{R, C\}$ receives superposition of both sources. Moreover the uninformed relay $\mathcal{R}_R$ also receives a signal from the informed one – $\mathcal{R}_C$ – separately. For $\mathcal{R}_i$ to $\mathcal{D}$ communication it is assumed for the sake of simplicity that the individual transmissions can be obtained separately at the $\mathcal{D}$. The half-duplex assumption forces the transmissions to occur in consecutive time slots.

Since WPLNC is assumed, each relay observes a superposition of incoming signals from both sources. Those observations may differ due to different parameters of the wireless links. Instead of distinguishing both individual sources the relay works with the overlapped signal as a whole. Relay processing – a decode and forward type – is generally given by a mapping

$$f_i : c_1 \times c_2 \to c_i, \tag{1}$$

where $i \in \{R, C\}$ denotes the relay, c_1, c_2 and c_i are symbols transmitted by $\mathcal{S}_1, \mathcal{S}_2$ and $\mathcal{R}_i$ respectively and $\times$ is Cartesian product. Notice that for simplicity we assume mapping over individual symbols not over whole codewords, which is also possible. The mapping is allowed to be many-to-one. In fact to utilise the gain of WPLNC it must be the many-to-one mapping.

When the WPLNC mapping f_i given by Eq.(1) is a *linear* one then the WPLNC operation of the relay can be described by matrix multiplication

$$\bar{c}_i = \mathbb{X}_i \begin{bmatrix} \bar{c}_1 \\ \bar{c}_2 \end{bmatrix}, \tag{2}$$

where $i \in \{R, C\}$ denotes the relay, $\bar{c}_1, \bar{c}_2$ and $\bar{c}_i$ are binary representations of symbols transmitted by $\mathcal{S}_1, \mathcal{S}_2$ and $\mathcal{R}_i$, respectively and $\mathbb{X}_i$ is binary matrix representing WPLNC mapping.

According to [8] we divide the WPLNC mappings f_i into several categories based on input and output cardinality relation. Assume a given source symbol cardinality $|c_1| = |c_2| = c$ then a mapping with cardinality $|c_i| = c$ will be denoted as a *minimal* one; XOR mapping is the well known example of the minimal mapping. A mapping with $|c_i| = c^2$ is denoted as a *full* one and every mapping in between those two bounds is denoted as an *extended* mapping. Note that even sub-minimal mappings with $|c_i| < c$ exist but they have limited usage in two relay networks, especially when we assume the symbol cardinalities to be the powers of 2.

According to the assumptions every destination node observes c_R and c_C symbols separately and wants to recover original source symbols c_1, c_2 from them. This is possible if and only if it is allowed by the properties of both relay mappings f_R and f_C, i.e. if and only if an inverse mapping exists at the destination $\mathcal{D}_j$:

$$f_j^{-1} : c_R \times c_C \to c_1 \times c_2. \tag{3}$$

If this inverse mapping exists for f_R, f_C we call the pair of them an *invertible pair*, otherwise it is a *non-invertible* pair.

In terms of presented matrix description (for linear WPLNC mappings only) the pair of mappings is invertible at $\mathcal{D}_j$ if and only if there exists a matrix $\mathbb{X}_j^{-1}$ such that

$$\begin{bmatrix} \bar{c}_1 \\ \bar{c}_2 \end{bmatrix} = \mathbb{X}_j^{-1} \begin{bmatrix} \bar{c}_R \\ \bar{c}_C \end{bmatrix}, \tag{4}$$

where $\bar{c}_i$ is the bit representation of appropriate symbol.

Invertibility of the pair of mappings $\mathbb{X}_R, \mathbb{X}_C$ can be easily checked by row rank (in GF(2) sense) of a matrix that is formed by a vertical concatenation of $\mathbb{X}_R$ and $\mathbb{X}_C$. Notice that any FULL mapping forms invertible pair with arbitrary WPLNC mapping.

In a centralised network the relay mappings f_i can be tailored to fit the situation properly, but this is not the case in distributed control scenarios. When the relays perform selfish selection of f_i, with lack of knowledge of the other relay actions, the invertibility of the source data may be violated since the inverse mapping in Eq.(3) may not exist. The situation is even more complicated when the relay behaviour depends on local conditions, such as a state of battery, that are not globally known to all the participating relays.

4   Sequential Game

We describe the situation of differently informed relays, that sequentially select their WPLNC mappings, as a sequential incomplete information game. Our game of interest is defined as follows: A set of players is $\mathcal{R}_C$ and $\mathcal{R}_R$. Relay node $\mathcal{R}_C$ has two possible incarnations – types – it has either high or low battery level. Type of the relay $\mathcal{R}_C$ is $t_C \in \{H, L\}$, where H denotes high battery level and L low level. Relay $\mathcal{R}_R$ has only one type, it always has full battery. The type t_C is a private information of $\mathcal{R}_C$ and is unknown to $\mathcal{R}_R$. A battery level is selected by nature prior to the beginning of the game. Low battery level is selected with probability p, this a priori probability is available to $\mathcal{R}_R$ too, but the actual battery level of $\mathcal{R}_C$ is not.

Each relay has a set of available actions, both sets contain various WPLNC mappings. To make the situation a bit easier we reduce the action set of $\mathcal{R}_R$ to two different minimal mappings MIN1 and MIN2 and a full mapping FULL. The action set of $\mathcal{R}_C$ depends on its type, high battery level type has the same action set as $\mathcal{R}_R$ since they are in fact the same. But low battery type uses minimal mappings only, i.e. its action set contains MIN1 and MIN2, this is because the minimal WPLNC mapping delivers data in the most energy saving way. For the sake of simplicity we do not assume EXT mappings in our example.

The relays are rewarded for the WPLNC mappings used. The payoff function is related to energy efficiency, since the MIN mappings compress the information more and thus save more energy. We define the payoff function as follows: at high battery level each node is more or less selfish, it tries to use the best (from its own point of view) possible mapping. Such a relay is awarded by $2A$ for using MIN1 mapping, by A for MIN2 and by B for full mapping, where $A > B > 0$. We assume without loss of generality that there are some minimal mappings that perform better (in terms of SER, etc.) in given channel conditions, that is why the rewards for various minimal mappings differ. We also assume that a minimal mapping is always better than a full mapping (from energy savings point of view). At low battery mode the relay $\mathcal{R}_C$ tries to deliver as much as possible information before its battery is depleted (ignoring any other performance measure, only energy efficiency matters). It is rewarded by $4A$ for any minimal mappings it uses, because of important energy savings. The relay $\mathcal{R}_R$, when facing low battery node, tries to help it and is rewarded by $4A$ for usage of full mapping since it helps most to $\mathcal{R}_C$ and by A for any invertible minimal mapping.

Whenever both relays select a pair of mappings that is non-invertible (see Eq.(3)) then the nodes waste their resources in vain and are penalised by $P \leq 0$ since they do not fulfil their task to enable $\mathcal{S}$ to $\mathcal{D}$ communication. Because wasting of resources is critical especially in low battery mode the relays are penalised by $2P$ when $\mathcal{R}_C$ is in low battery state. The payoff matrices of both game incarnations are given in Tabs. 1 and 2.

Table 1. Payoff matrix for high battery vs. high battery game.

	MIN1	MIN2	FULL
MIN1	P,P	2A,A	2A,B
MIN2	A,2A	P,P	A,B
FULL	B,2A	B,A	B,B

Table 2. Payoff matrix for high battery vs. low battery game.

	MIN1	MIN2
MIN1	2P,2P	2A,4A
MIN2	A,4A	2P,2P
FULL	4A,4A	4A,4A

The uniformed player can form beliefs about the informed one based on observed actions and a priori type probability, e.g. after observing MIN1 mapping the $\mathcal{R}_R$ can create a belief $\mu(H|MIN1)$ of $\mathcal{R}_C$ being type H. The belief system is important when evaluating expected utilities and when searching for the game equilibria.

The game sequence and rules are depicted in Fig.2. The dashed regions show common information sets, e.g. the relay $\mathcal{R}_R$ is unsure about the type of $\mathcal{R}_C$ when it observes MIN1 mapping, it has only belief about the type, so both paths leading to MIN1 dashed region belong to the same information set. It can be also seen that FULL mapping is a singleton information set since it automatically means that $t_C = H$. Edges that represent relays' actions are from left to right MIN1, MIN2 and FULL. Rewards are shown at the leaves of the game tree, $\mathcal{R}_C$'s upper and $\mathcal{R}_R$'s lower.

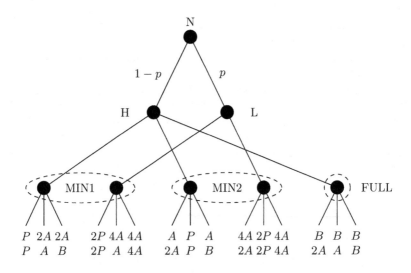

Fig. 2. Game tree of sequential game

5   Equilibria Analysis and Discussion

The proposed game is called a sequential incomplete information game. Also, due to presence of signalisation link, a signalling game. Widely accepted solution for this type of games is Perfect Bayesian Equilibrium (PBE) [12]. A PBE is a strategy profile $s^* = (a_C^*, a_R^*)$ and a belief system μ^* such that the strategies are sequentially rational given the belief system and the belief system is consistent given the strategy profile. Sequential rationality means that the action taken in given information set is optimal given the belief and actions of the other players.

Consistent belief systems means that the beliefs at least in the information sets on-the-equilibrium-path are given by Bayes' rule.

Since the relay $\mathcal{R}_C$ has two possible types its strategy is a doublet assigning an action to both types, e.g. $a_C = (a_C(H), a_C(L)) = (\text{MIN1}, \text{MIN2})$ means that $\mathcal{R}_C$ of type $t_C = H$ uses MIN1 while type $t_C = L$ plays MIN2. When the action played by different types is the same we call this a pooling strategy, otherwise it is a separating strategy.

In the proposed game there four separating:

$$a_C = (a_C(H), a_C(L)) = (\text{MIN1}, \text{MIN2})$$
$$a_C = (a_C(H), a_C(L)) = (\text{MIN2}, \text{MIN1})$$
$$a_C = (a_C(H), a_C(L)) = (\text{MIN1}, \text{FULL})$$
$$a_C = (a_C(H), a_C(L)) = (\text{MIN2}, \text{FULL}),$$

and two pooling strategies of $\mathcal{R}_C$:

$$a_C = (a_C(H), a_C(L)) = (\text{MIN1}, \text{MIN1})$$
$$a_C = (a_C(H), a_C(L)) = (\text{MIN2}, \text{MIN2})$$

Since $\mathcal{R}_R$ has only one type its strategy is a singleton action a_R such as $a_R = \text{MIN1}$.

Proposition 1. *The only PBEs of the proposed games are connected with the pooling strategy $a_C^* = (a_C^*(H), a_C^*(L)) = (MIN1, MIN1)$. Otherwise there is no PBE.*

Proof. To prove the Proposition 1 we have to show that there is a consistent belief system and sequentially rational strategies for both players. First of all define belief system: on the equilibrium path $\mathcal{R}_R$'s belief about $\mathcal{R}_C$ having high battery level after observing MIN1 is $\mu(H|\text{MIN1}) = 1 - p$ which follows from Bayesian rule. Off the equilibrium path beliefs should be undefined such as $\mu(H|\text{MIN2})$ but due to singleton information set of FULL mapping the belief $\mu(H|\text{FULL})$ is simply 1. Thus the belief system is consistent given a_C^*.

Having the consistent belief system we show the sequential rationality of the strategy. We first seek the best responses of $\mathcal{R}_R$ on observed signals from $\mathcal{R}_C$ having $\mathcal{R}_R$'s beliefs. The expected payoff of $\mathcal{R}_R$ obtained in response to $a_C = \text{MIN1}$ for all three actions of $\mathcal{R}_R$ is:

$$\text{MIN1:} \quad (1 - p)P + p2P = P - pP$$
$$\text{MIN2:} \quad (1 - p)A + pA = A$$
$$\text{FULL:} \quad (1 - p)B + p4A = B - pB + p4A$$

Thus the $\mathcal{R}_R$'s best response on action $a_C = \text{MIN1}$ is $a_R = \text{MIN2}$ if $p < \frac{A-B}{4A-B}$ or $a_R = \text{FULL}$ elsewhere, of course $p \in [0, 1]$.

The $\mathcal{R}_R$'s best response on action $a_C = \text{MIN2}$ is undefined since the belief $\mu(H|\text{MIN2})$ is not defined. Later we will refer to this potential best response as $a_R(\text{MIN2})$.

The $\mathcal{R}_R$'s best response on action $a_C = $ FULL is $a_R = $ MIN1 simply because $2A > A > B$, see Fig.2.

Knowing the best response of $\mathcal{R}_R$, the strategy of $\mathcal{R}_C$ and belief system the assumed strategy is PBE if and only if $\mathcal{R}_C$ has no incentive to change its strategy, i.e. its expected payoff should be the highest among all possible alternative strategies. Let us start with the situation when the best response on $a_C = $ MIN1 is $a_R = $ MIN2. Then the expected payoff of $\mathcal{R}_C$ must be:

$$\pi_C(H, \text{MIN1}, \text{MIN2}) \geq \pi_C(H, \text{FULL}, \text{MIN1}) \tag{5}$$

$$\pi_C(H, \text{MIN1}, \text{MIN2}) \geq \pi_C(H, \text{MIN2}, a_R(\text{MIN2})) \tag{6}$$

$$\pi_C(L, \text{MIN1}, \text{MIN2}) \geq \pi_C(L, \text{MIN2}, a_R(\text{MIN2})), \tag{7}$$

where $\pi_C(t_C, a_C, a_R)$ is payoff of $\mathcal{R}_C$ of type t_C playing action a_C while $\mathcal{R}_R$ plays a_R. All equations are true since (5) is $2A \geq B$, (6) is $2A \geq A$ since A is maximal possible payoff of $\mathcal{R}_C$ given that strategy and (7) is $4A \geq 4A$ since $4A$ is maximal possible payoff of $\mathcal{R}_C$ given that strategy.

Secondly, assume that the best response on $a_C = $ MIN1 is $a_R = $ FULL. Then the expected payoff of $\mathcal{R}_C$ must be:

$$\pi_C(H, \text{MIN1}, \text{FULL}) \geq \pi_C(H, \text{FULL}, \text{MIN1}) \tag{8}$$

$$\pi_C(H, \text{MIN1}, \text{FULL}) \geq \pi_C(H, \text{MIN2}, a_R(\text{MIN2})) \tag{9}$$

$$\pi_C(L, \text{MIN1}, \text{FULL}) \geq \pi_C(L, \text{MIN2}, a_R(\text{MIN2})). \tag{10}$$

All equations are true since (8) is $2A \geq C$, (9) is $2A \geq A$ since A is maximal possible payoff of $\mathcal{R}_C$ given that strategy and (10) is $4A \geq 4A$ since $4A$ is maximal possible payoff of $\mathcal{R}_C$ given that strategy.

This holds true for arbitrary belief $\mu(H|\text{MIN2}) \in [0, 1]$. We have shown that there are two PBEs based on mutual relation between A, B and $p - s_1^* = (a_C^*(H), a_C^*(L), a_R^*) = (\text{MIN1}, \text{MIN1}, \text{MIN2})$ and $s_2^* = (a_C^*(H), a_C^*(L), a_R^*) = (\text{MIN1}, \text{MIN1}, \text{FULL})$ with belief system $\mu^*(H|\text{MIN1}) = 1 - p$, $\mu^*(H|\text{MIN2}) \in [0, 1]$ and $\mu^*(H|\text{FULL}) = 1$. s_1^* is PBE if $p < \frac{A-B}{4A-B}$ otherwise it is s_2^*.

By similar reasoning it can be shown that aforementioned pooling strategy of $\mathcal{R}_C$ is the only PBE of the proposed game. ∎

Fig.3 shows a surface that divides regions of existence of both PBE. Below this surface s_1^* is the PBE of the game, above it is s_2^*. The surface is given by probability of low battery state $p = \frac{A-B}{4A-B}$ as a function of rewards A, B. It can be concluded that the higher the probability of depleted battery and the higher the reward B the relay $\mathcal{R}_R$ will prefer action FULL since it supports $\mathcal{R}_C$ and provides the higher payoff.

6   Conclusions

In this paper we have proposed a sequential incomplete information game between the relays in wireless network. As an example of globally unknown information we focused on battery state of one of the relays. The battery level affects

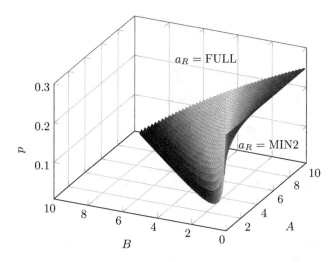

Fig. 3. Regions of existence of individual PBEs

the actions taken by that relay which consequently determines the performance of the whole network. The other relay has a chance to observe the battery state only through observing the actions taken. This relay can potentially modify its operation to improve the performance and to support the node with low battery.

We show that such a game possesses some Perfect Bayesian Equilibria that provide reasonable prediction of the game results that tends to reliable sources to destinations communications. Moreover the relay with emptying battery delivers the information in energy efficient way.

Acknowledgement. Work in this paper was supported by the European Science Foundation through FP7-ICT DIWINE project, the Ministry of Education, Youth and Sports of the Czech Republic grant LD12062 and by the Grant Agency of the Czech Technical University in Prague SGS15/090/OHK3/1T/13.

References

1. Zhang, S., Liew, S.C., Lam, P.P.: Hot topic: physical-layer network coding. In: Proceedings of the 12th Annual International Conference on Mobile Computing and Networking, MobiCom 2006, New York, NY, USA, pp. 358–365. ACM (2006)
2. Ahlswede, R., Cai, N., Li, S.-Y., Yeung, R.: Network information flow. IEEE Transactions on Information Theory **46**(4), 1204–1216 (2000)
3. Rankov, B., Wittneben, A.: Achievable rate regions for the two-way relay channel. In: Proc. IEEE Int. Symposium on Information Theory (ISIT), July 2006. http://www.nari.ee.ethz.ch/wireless/pubs/p/isit2006
4. Katti, S., Gollakota, S., Katabi, D.: Embracing wireless interference: Analog network coding. SIGCOMM Comput. Commun. Rev. **37**(4), 397–408 (2007)

5. Nazer, B., Gastpar, M.: Compute-and-forward: Harnessing interference through structured codes. IEEE Transactions on Information Theory **57**(10), 6463–6486 (2011)
6. Popovski, P., Yomo, H.: Bi-directional amplification of throughput in a wireless multi-hop network. In: IEEE 63rd Vehicular Technology Conference, VTC 2006-Spring, vol. 2, pp. 588–593, May 2006
7. Katti, S., Rahul, H., Hu, W., Katabi, D., Medard, M., Crowcroft, J.: XORs in the air: Practical wireless network coding. IEEE/ACM Transactions on Networking **16**(3), 497–510 (2008)
8. Sykora, J., Burr, A.: Layered design of hierarchical exclusive codebook and its capacity regions for HDF strategy in parametric wireless 2-WRC. IEEE Transactions on Vehicular Technology **60**(7), 3241–3252 (2011)
9. Wang, W., Chatterjee, M., Kwiat, K.: Coexistence with malicious nodes: a game theoretic approach. In: International Conference on Game Theory for Networks, GameNets 2009, pp. 277–286, May 2009
10. Dehnie, S., Sencar, H., Memon, N.: Detecting malicious behavior in cooperative diversity. In: 41st Annual Conference on Information Sciences and Systems, CISS 2007, pp. 895–899, March 2007
11. Chen, M.-H., Lin, S.-C., Hong, Y.-W.: A game theoretic approach for the cooperative network with the presence of malicious relays. In: 2011 IEEE Global Telecommunications Conference (GLOBECOM 2011), pp. 1–5, December 2011
12. Fudenberg, D., Tirole, J.: Game Theory. MIT Press (1991)

Device-to-Device Data Storage
with Regenerating Codes

Joonas Pääkkönen[1]([✉]), Camilla Hollanti[1], and Olav Tirkkonen[2]

[1] Department of Mathematics and Systems Analysis, School of Science,
Aalto University, Espoo, Finland
{joonas.paakkonen,camilla.hollanti}@aalto.fi
[2] Department of Communications and Networking, School of Electrical Engineering,
Aalto University, Espoo, Finland
olav.tirkkonen@aalto.fi

Abstract. Caching data files directly on mobile user devices combined
with device-to-device (D2D) communications has recently been suggested
to improve the capacity of wireless networks. We investigate the performance of regenerating codes in terms of the total energy consumption of
a cellular network. We show that regenerating codes can offer large performance gains. It turns out that using redundancy against storage node
failures is only beneficial if the popularity of the data is between certain
thresholds. As our major contribution, we investigate under which circumstances regenerating codes with multiple redundant data fragments
outdo uncoded caching.

1 Introduction

As the amount of mobile data traffic is predicted to keep growing rapidly in
the near future [1], more efficient data transmission and distribution methods
are needed. Mobile video traffic has quickly become one of the most important
factors straining the already burdened cellular networks. As video files are often
large, they typically incur significant stress on both cellular networks and backhaul links. Thus, moving traffic away from the traditional cellular and backhaul
links could drastically reduce the strain on these links. Further, finding cost-
efficient solutions to deliver large, popular data files is important for minimizing
the energy consumption of data transmission.

We have observed that the storage space of mobile devices has been increasing.
This leads us to the following question: how could we utilize this storage capacity
to improve wireless networks? One idea is to use this storage to cache files and
distribute them directly between users.

Recently, distributing data directly from devices through device-to-device
(D2D) communication has been studied in [3–5]. Principal work on caching as
a prefetching method has been conducted in [11,13], whereas seminal work on
distributed caching, particularly for D2D networks, has been done in [10]. While
coding has been suggested to improve the performance of caching systems [6–9],

© Springer International Publishing Switzerland 2015
M. Jonsson et al. (Eds.): MACOM 2015, LNCS 9305, pp. 57–69, 2015.
DOI: 10.1007/978-3-319-23440-3_5

most of the work in the literature offers no solution to keep the cached files available even when the caching devices move out of coverage.

In this paper, we investigate how redundancy could be used to ensure file availability within a designated area – even if some nodes *fail*, i.e. leave the area and become unavailable. Namely, we study the performance of regenerating codes [15] that are codes designed specifically for distributed storage. For further reading, e.g. [14] provides an overview of these codes.

We are interested in the performance of the minimum storage regenerating (MSR) and the minimum bandwidth regenerating (MBR) codes, which lie on the far ends of the storage-bandwidth tradeoff curve [15,16]. The performance is measured in terms of the expected total transmission cost of the system. Unlike our prior work on similar problems [17,18], the current paper assumes both infinite storage capacities on the users, and that the system must be able to cope with multiple simultaneous failures. That is, even if several users leave the coverage area, the data should still remain available for download from the storage nodes.

We find that the popularity of the file, the number of users, and the transmission costs all have an effect on which storage method should be chosen. With the help of numerical results, we characterize the decision rules on choosing the optimal method.

2   System Model

The current work is based on three key assumptions. Firstly, we assume that mobile user devices have plenty of free storage capacity that can be used to store data. Secondly, we assume that these devices can be used to distribute the stored data to other users via perfect, error-free D2D links. Thirdly, we assume that, on average, transmitting data between mobile devices is less expensive than transmitting data from a base station to a user. This assumption is mostly motivated by the path loss laws of wireless signals, i.e. more transmit power is needed to transmit signals over longer distances. We assume that the average distance between a user and the base station is larger than the average distance between any two nodes.

Based on these assumptions, we show that storing data files with redundancy can lead to significant cost savings. Furthermore, we find explicit thresholds for choosing the most appropriate file storage method given the system parameters.

In our system model, users stay in the system for a random, exponentially distributed amount of time with expected value T. We say that the rate at which users pass through the system is $\lambda = \frac{1}{T}$, which can be also thought of as the expected node failure rate.

We denote the expected number of nodes in the system by N. We assume that the instantaneous number of nodes can be described by the M/M/∞ Markov model, shown in Fig. 1, where the state corresponds to the instantaneous number of nodes. It is well-known that the probability that this chain is in state i is [2]

$$\pi(i) = \frac{N^i}{i!} e^{-N}.$$ (1)

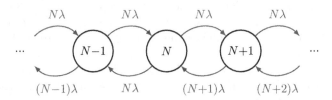

Fig. 1. M/M/∞ Markov chain state diagram for the instantaneous number of nodes (blue). The incoming rate (green) of the nodes is constant, whereas the outgoing rate (red) is proportional to the number of nodes in the system. The expected number of nodes is N and $\lambda = 1/T$.

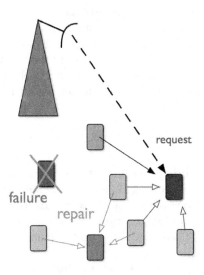

Fig. 2. Node requesting (blue) a file can be served by the base station (grey), a single storage node (green, simple caching or replication), or by a set of storage nodes each transmitting an encoded data block. When a node fails (red), the lost block can be repaired to a new node (magenta). Here $d = k = 3$.

Without loss of generality, let there be one file of size $B = 1$. Let us assume that each user that is connected to the system requests the file at random, exponentially distributed time intervals with expected value $\tau = \frac{1}{\omega}$, where ω is called the *file request rate*.

We assume that files are always available, either from the base station or from a set of storage nodes. Let $R > 1$ denote the expected cost ratio between transmitting a bit from the base station and transmitting a bit from another user through a D2D link. That is, the cost of retrieving the file from the base station is R, while the cost of retrieving the file from another user is only 1. Note that R could be either based on measurements, or it could be artificially set by the system designer to adjust the amount of traffic offloaded from the base station to the D2D connections. The higher the value of R, the more traffic is moved away from the base station.

Additionally, let $p = \omega T = \frac{\omega}{\lambda}$ be the expected number of requests that one user generates during the time it spends in the system. As it is reasonable to assume that users do not generally request a certain file more than once during their visit to the system, we mainly focus on the case $p < 1$.

Fig. 2 illustrates the system setup and the select data storage and distribution methods along with the repair process, which we discuss in more detail in the following section.

3   Analysis

In this section, we introduce the three storage methods used throughout the paper: simple caching, regenerating codes and replication. We derive closed-form expressions for the expected total cost per time unit for each of them. We note that traditional erasure coding and retrieving data directly from the base station cannot outperform MSR and simple caching, respectively. For this reason, we do not consider these two methods. This is further justified in detail later in this section.

3.1   Simple Caching

We call the method of storing one full copy of the data file on a single node with no redundancy *simple caching*. As long as the node that is caching the file stays in the system, all file requests lead to retrievals from this node. There are, on average, $(N - 1)$ nodes that generate requests as the node storing the file does not request the file. Therefore, the expected number of requests during the lifetime of the caching node is $(N - 1)p$.

If the caching node fails, the next node that requests the file has to download it from the base station. The expected time in which this happens is $\frac{1}{N\omega}$ as the expected total request rate is $N\omega$. Therefore, the expected time in which a number of $(N - 1)\omega T + 1$ requests are generated is $T + \frac{1}{N\omega}$. The expected cost of these requests is $(N - 1)\omega T + R$ and, thereby, the expected cost of simple caching becomes[1]

$$C_{\text{sc}} = \frac{(N - 1)\omega T + R}{T + \frac{1}{N\omega}} = \frac{(N - 1)\omega + R\lambda}{1 + \frac{\lambda}{N\omega}}. \tag{2}$$

It should be noted that if we only serve file requests from the base station, the expected cost becomes $RN\omega$. It is easy to see that this method cannot beat simple caching, i.e. $C_{\text{sc}} < RN\omega$, for all $R > 1$. This is due to the fact that part of the requests of simple caching are served by a cheaper D2D connection. Thus, we do not consider the method of serving users only via the base station.

3.2   Redundant Caching with Regenerating Codes

Here we use regenerating codes [15] with n storage nodes to ensure file availability. Regenerating codes with parameters (n, k, d) are maximum distance separable (MDS) codes that allow any k nodes to be contacted to recover the file. Furthermore, regenerating codes possess the so called *reconstruction property*, which says that contacting any d nodes allows resurrecting a lost node. Throughout this work, we call k the reconstruction degree and d the repair degree.

There are two extreme cases of regenerating codes: the minimum storage regenerating (MSR) code and the minimum bandwidth regenerating (MBR) code. For example [16] provides code constructions for both the MBR and the MSR point. The MSR code minimizes the number of data stored on the storage nodes, while the MBR code minimizes the amount of traffic required when repairing a lost data block. Here the amount of information stored on each node is denoted α, and the amount of information communicated at each repair is denoted γ. In [15], the values of α and γ for MBR and MSR were derived to yield

$$(\alpha_{\text{MBR}}, \gamma_{\text{MBR}}) = \left(\frac{2Bd}{2kd - k^2 + k}, \frac{2Bd}{2kd - k^2 + k} \right) \tag{3}$$

$$(\alpha_{\text{MSR}}, \gamma_{\text{MSR}}) = \left(\frac{B}{k}, \frac{Bd}{k(d - k + 1)} \right), \tag{4}$$

where B is the file size, which we set to $B = 1$ in this work without loss of generality.

It should be noted that the MSR code with $d = k$ is equivalent to traditional MDS erasure coding. Furthermore, when $d > k$, MSR outperforms traditional

---

[1] Note that the expected value of the ratio of two random variables is not generally equal to the quotient of the expected values of these variables. Nonetheless, (2) has been shown give a very good approximation of C_{sc} through computer simulations. Similar approximations are used for other expected values of ratios and products throughout this paper.

MDS coding because of its lower repair bandwidth. Thus, we do not consider traditional erasure coding as a separate coding method in this work.

Even though the MBR code minimizes the amount of traffic required when a node becomes unavailable and its contents must be regenerated to another node, the storage space needed for MBR is higher than that of MSR. In view of the current work, more importantly, the reconstruction bandwidth is higher for MBR than for MSR. That is, MBR requires more information than the size of the file to be transmitted every time a user requests the file. Therefore, whether to apply MBR or MSR, or either, largely depends on the time users spend in the system, and the popularity of the file.

Now we derive the exact expression for the cost function for regenerating codes as a function of parameters $R, N, \omega, \lambda, n, k$ and d. These expressions are general in terms of the repair bandwidth γ and the size of the stored block α. Thereby, the expressions can be used for both the MSR and the MBR code – only the values of γ and α must be changed.

We divide the expected total cost expression of regenerating codes into six costs: allocation cost C_1, cost of creating redundancy C_2, repair cost C_3, cost of remote retrievals C_4, cost of data reconstruction by storage nodes C_5, and cost of data reconstruction with many nodes C_6. In the following, we further explain these cost terms and present the expected cost of each term.

Allocation cost: Each time there are exactly $k-1$ nodes and a new node enters the system, which happens with probability $\pi(k-1)\frac{N}{k-1+N}$, the base station allocates a block of size α to all k nodes. Note that, to get the expected cost over time, this cost must be normalized by the expected time that a user spends in the system, which is simply $\sum_{i=0}^{\infty} \left(\frac{T}{i+N}\right) \pi(i) = \frac{1}{2N\lambda}$. Thus, the expected cost of reallocation after data loss becomes

$$C_1 = 2N\lambda\pi(k-1)\left(\frac{N}{k-1+N}\right)Rk\alpha.$$

Cost of creating redundancy: This process creates the desired redundant data blocks. If the number of nodes is in $[k, d-1]$ when a new node appears, we transmit $k\alpha$ bits to the new node, while if the number of nodes is in $[d, n-1]$, we only need to communicate γ bits. This cost becomes

$$C_2 = 2N\lambda\sum_{i=k}^{d-1}\pi(i)\left(\frac{N}{i+N}\right)k\alpha + 2N\lambda\sum_{i=d}^{n-1}\pi(i)\left(\frac{N}{i+N}\right)\gamma.$$

Repair cost: Every time a storage node leaves the system, the system attempts to repair the lost block of data in order to keep the number of stored blocks constant. The probability that there are i nodes, and that the next event is a node departure, and that the departed node was storing a block is $\pi(i)\frac{i}{i+N}\frac{n}{i}$. Repairing is only possible if there is at least one empty node after the departure of a storage node. Thus, we sum over $i \in [n+2, \infty)$. The cost of each repair is γ, so the repair cost becomes

$$C_3 = 2N\lambda \sum_{i=n+2}^{\infty} \pi(i) \left(\frac{i}{i+N}\right) \left(\frac{n}{i}\right) \gamma$$

$$= 2N\lambda \sum_{i=n+2}^{\infty} \pi(i) \frac{n\gamma}{i+N}.$$

Cost of remote retrievals: If there are fewer than k nodes, the base station must be contacted to download the file. This cost becomes

$$C_4 = \sum_{i=1}^{k-1} \pi(i) i w R.$$

Cost of reconstruction by storage nodes: If the number of nodes is in $[k, n]$, every time a node requests a file, it only needs to connect to $k-1$ other nodes since it already has one block stored on itself. Thus, this cost becomes

$$C_5 = \sum_{i=k}^{n} \pi(i) i w (k-1) \alpha.$$

Cost of data reconstruction with many nodes: If there are more than n nodes, the n nodes that are already storing a block only need to connect to $k-1$ nodes for reconstruction, while the nodes that are not storing anything must connect to k nodes. The cost of these requests becomes

$$C_6 = \sum_{i=n+1}^{\infty} \pi(i) n w (k-1) \alpha + \sum_{i=n+1}^{\infty} \pi(i)(i-n) w k \alpha$$

$$= \sum_{i=n+1}^{\infty} \pi(i)(ki-n) \alpha w.$$

Note that, although not shown in the above equations, α and γ are functions of k and d, just like in (3) and (4).

The performance metric in which we are interested, i.e. the expected total cost, becomes the sum of all the above six costs. However, if the average number of nodes is much higher than the average number of nodes storing a data block, i.e. if $N \gg n$, only the repair cost C_3 and the reconstruction cost with many nodes C_6 count since all the other events become extremely rare. Nevertheless, in the numerical results of this work, we take all the six events into consideration.

3.3 Replication

When replication is used, n nodes store an exact replica of the data file. If we set $k = \alpha = \gamma = 1$, we can use the sum of all the six expressions of regenerating codes in the previous section to find the cost of the replication method. While replication is simple and has a minimum reconstruction bandwidth, its drawback is its high repair bandwidth. Additionally, replication consumes plenty of storage space. This, however, is not important here as we assume that all nodes have very large storage capacities.

We point out that the expressions for the cost of simple caching, caching with regenerating codes, and replication could be used to analytically find the best method for given system parameters. Due to the laborious nature of this task and the lack of space, however, we only find the optimal methods with the help of numerical computations. Additionally, it is important to note that finding the optimal method analytically only yields inequations of $p = \frac{\omega}{\lambda}$, i.e. only the ratio of ω and λ matters, not the actual values.

4   Numerical Results

It may be desirable that the number of storage nodes that participate in the repair and reconstruction processes in a distributed storage system is high because high reconstruction and repair degrees imply low transmission costs. However, for our system setup, we intentionally keep the number of participating nodes relatively low. We limit the values of parameters k and d to a certain maximum. This is because, in practice, it can be very difficult to establish a large number of simultaneous D2D links whenever a user wants to reconstruct the file, or when a failed node must be repaired.

Setting up several parallel data streams could speed up the download process, which would motivate keeping k and d relatively large. The faster the D2D link to a certain node is, the more data could be retrieved from that node. However, both parallel and asymmetric downloads are outside of the scope of this paper, but they could be investigated in future work.

For the numerical analysis of this section, we set the maximum repair degree to $d = 10$. More precisely, we will always use $d = 10$ as it is obvious from (3) and (4) that maximizing d minimizes both α and γ. Further, fixing $d = 10$ implies that $k \in [2, 10]$, as $2 \le k \le d$.

Even though here it is sensible to limit the values of k and d, it is beneficial to keep the number of storage nodes n relatively high. Here we set $n = 30$, which we consider to be high enough to avoid losing the file too easily due to potential multiple simultaneous failures, but still low enough so that we can assume that the average number of nodes is much less than the desired number of storage nodes, i.e. $n \ll N$. In practice, the value of n would affect the data transmission cost ratio R. If the downloading node can choose the k or d closest nodes to contact, it would always be beneficial to have n as high as possible. However, in this work, we ignore this effect due to its complex nature and note that this could be another direction of future work.

4.1   Finding the Optimal Method

Finding the method that yields the minimum cost is rather complicated because of the large number of both system parameters and code parameters. We need

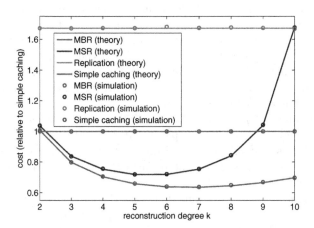

Fig. 3. Costs of regenerating codes relative to simple caching as functions of k with $R = 20$, $N = 1000$, and $p = 0.005 \approx 10^{-2.3}$ (cf. Fig. 4). Here MBR with $k = 7$ yields the best performance. Simple caching and replication are independent of k, but the simulations are repeated for each point on the lines.

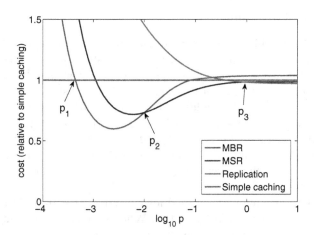

Fig. 4. Costs as a function of the expected number of file requests during the lifetime of a node (p) for $R = 20$ and $N = 1000$. Here both MBR and MSR can yield significant savings, while replication only offers modest improvements for very high request rates. The arrows point to the crossing points of the corresponding curves, i.e. the switching thresholds for p.

to compare the cost of simple caching and replication to the minimum costs of MBR and MSR. Fig. 3 suggests that finding the optimal k is not trivial. The same figure shows that the gains are notable, especially when using the MBR code with $k = 7$ in this example.

Figure 4 shows the optimal performances of each method as functions of $p = \frac{\omega}{\lambda}$. For extremely low values of p, the number of failures is large compared to the number of file requests. Therefore, the repair cost vastly dominates the total cost, and it is not worth repairing the file if the request rate is too low. Consequently, simple caching is the desired method here. One might also argue that, in the case of a very low request rate, caching would imply such small cost savings that it should not be used at all.

For higher values of p, the number of file requests justifies the use of distributed storage on the nodes but repairs still dominate the total cost. Therefore, MBR performs best in this case. However, further increasing p means that it becomes more and more important to keep the file reconstruction cost low, thus, MSR should be chosen.

For a very high p, reconstructions dominate the total cost. Even though the reconstruction cost of MSR is equal to that of replication, replication performs better as it reduces the total request rate. When MSR is used, even the storage nodes that are storing data must download the remaining $k - 1$ blocks in order to recover the data file. On the contrary, when replication is used, all of the n storage nodes are already storing the file, so they do not need to download anything.

4.2   Switching Thresholds

In the remainder of this section we present switching thresholds for certain parameter values. For example, the switching threshold p_1 for choosing MBR over simple caching means that if $p > p_1$, then MBR should be chosen over simple caching because it yields a lower expected total cost.

Fig. 5 shows switching thresholds p_1 for choosing MBR over simple caching. The switching thresholds are presented for (R, N) parameter pairs with $R \in [20, 180]$ and $N \in [10^2, 10^5]$. Finding a good curve fit for the surface of Fig. 5 turns out to be rather complicated, and we leave this outside of the scope of this paper. Nonetheless, we find a very simple curve fit for p_2 and present it later in this section.

We see that the switching threshold for choosing MBR over simple caching (p_1) seems to decrease with both R and N. When we increase R, contacting the base station becomes more and more expensive. When we increase N, the total request rate of the file increases. We see that for high values of R or N, it is important to keep the file available on the nodes as we want to avoid having to contact the base station.

According to our simulation results, it turns out that we can find a very simple approximation for the threshold for choosing MSR over MBR: $p_2 \approx \frac{10}{N}$. Here p_2 is practically independent of R and only decreases with N. This is because it is very unlikely that we need to contact the base station when using either MBR or MSR since $k \ll N$, i.e. it is very unlikely that the number of nodes drops below k, which would mean that reconstructing the file is not possible and that we would need to contact the base station. When N increases, so does the expected

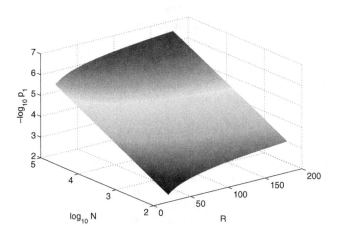

Fig. 5. Thresholds for switching from simple caching to MBR, i.e. MBR should be used if $p > p_1$. The threshold decreases with both the cost ratio R and the expected number of nodes N. Higher z-coordinate on the surface means lower p_1.

total request rate of the file, which means that efficient reconstruction becomes increasingly important, and MSR is thus desired.

The threshold for choosing replication over MSR (p_3) seems to remain constant at approximately $p_3 = 0.90$. Again, it is very unlikely that we need to contact the base station when we use either MSR or replication, and the value of R does not matter. As switching from MSR to replication only matters to the nodes that are storing data, and as we keep the number of these nodes constant at n, changing N does not affect the decision threshold p_3.

It should be noted that all these results hold verbatim only for $n = 30$, $k = 2, 3, ..., 10$ and $d = 10$. Nevertheless, according to our numerical results, the decision thresholds behave in a similar manner for many other values of n, k, d as well. Therefore, we claim that the behaviour exhibited in these figures also applies to more general settings. However, if the number of storage nodes n is set too high, regenerating codes should not be used. This is because a high value of n incurs a high number of failures and repairs, i.e. a high repair cost. Thus, it is crucial that the system designer chooses well-adjusted values for n, k, and d, which means finding a balance between the number of simultaneous failures that the system needs to withstand, and the expected number of repairs.

5   Conclusions

We have investigated the performance of regenerating codes with many redundant data blocks, caching without redundancy, and replication in a D2D caching system. We have shown that coded storage can offer significant cost savings compared to uncoded storage. We have characterized the decision rules on choosing the optimal method. Coding should only be used if the popularity of the file is between certain thresholds. For very low popularity, no redundancy is required. For very high popularity, replication should be used.

Acknowledgments. This work was supported in part by the Finnish Funding Agency for Innovation (TEKES) under grant no. 40142/13, and the Academy of Finland (grants #276031, #282938, and #283262). The support from the European Science Foundation under the COST Action IC1104 is also gratefully acknowledged.

References

1. Cisco, Cisco Visual Networking Index: Global Mobile Data Traffic Forecast Update, 2013–2018, (2014). White Paper. http://goo.gl/l77HAJ
2. Harrison, P., Patel, N.M.: Performance Modelling of Communication Networks and Computer Architectures, p. 173. Addison-Wesley (1992)
3. Han, T., Ansari, N.: Offloading Mobile Traffic via Green Content Broker. IEEE Internet of Things Journal **1**(2), 161–170 (2014)
4. Li, Y., Wang, Z., Jin, D., Chen, S.: Optimal Mobile Content Downloading in Device-to-Device Communication Underlaying Cellular Networks. IEEE Transactions on Wireless Communications **13**(7), 3596–3608 (2014)
5. Golrezaei, N., Mansourifard, P., Molisch, A.F., Dimakis, A.G.: Base Station Assisted Device-to-Device Communications for High-Throughput Wireless Video Networks. IEEE Transactions on Wireless Communications **13**(7), 3665–3676 (2014)
6. Hachem, J., Karamchandani, N., Diggavi, S.: Coded Caching for Heterogeneous Wireless Networks with Multi-level Access, arXiv:1404.6560 (2014)
7. Li, Y., et al.: Coding or Not: Optimal Mobile Data Offloading in Opportunistic Vehicular Networks. IEEE Transactions on Intelligent Transportation Systems **15**(1), 318–333 (2014)
8. Monteiro, J.G.: Modeling and Analysis of Reliable Peer-to-Peer Storage Systems, Ph.D. dissertation, CNRS, Uni. Nice-Sophia Antipolis (2010)
9. Golrezaei, N., Shanmugam, K., Dimakis, A.G., Molisch, A.F., Caire, G.: Femto-Caching: Wireless Video Content Delivery through Distributed Caching Helpers. IEEE Transactions on Information Theory **59**(12), 8402–8413 (2013)
10. Ji, M., Caire, G., Molisch, A.F.: Fundamental limits of distributed caching in d2d wireless networks. In: Proc. IEEE Information Theory Workshop (ITW), pp. 1–5 (2013)
11. Baştuğ, E., Bennis, M., Debbah, M.: Living on the Edge: The Role of Proactive Caching in 5G Wireless Networks. IEEE Communications Magazine **52**(8), 82–89 (2014)
12. Blasiak, A., Kleinberg, R., Lubetzky, E.: Broadcasting With Side Information: Bounding and Approximating the Broadcast Rate. IEEE Transactions on Information Theory **59**(9), 5811–5823 (2013)
13. Maddah-Ali, M.A., Niesen, U.: Fundamental Limits of Caching. IEEE Transactions on Information Theory **60**(5), 2856–2867 (2014)
14. Datta, A., Oggier, F.: An Overview of Codes Tailor-made for Networked Distributed Data Storage. Association for Computing Machinery Special Interest Group on Algorithms and Computation Theory News **44**(1), 89–105 (2013)
15. Dimakis, A.G., Godfrey, P.B., Wu, Y., Wainwright, M.O., Ramchandran, K.: Network Coding for Distributed Storage Systems. IEEE Transactions on Information Theory **56**(9), 4539–4551 (2010)

16. Rashmi, K.V., Shah, N.B., Kumar, P.V.: Optimal Exact-Regenerating Codes for Distributed Storage at the MSR and MBR Points via a Product-Matrix Construction. IEEE Transactions on Information Theory **57**(8), 5227–5239 (2011)
17. Pääkkönen, J., Dharmawansa, P., Hollanti, C., Tirkkonen, O.: Distributed storage for proximity based services. In: Proc. IEEE Swedish Communication Technologies Workshop, pp. 30–35 (2012)
18. Pääkkönen, J., Hollanti, C., Tirkkonen, O.: Device-to-device data storage for mobile cellular systems. In: Proc. IEEE Globecom Workshops, pp. 671–676 (2013)

A Random Access Protocol Incorporating Multi-packet Reception, Retransmission Diversity and Successive Interference Cancellation

Ramiro Samano-Robles[1]([⊠]), Desmond C. McLernon[2], and Mounir Ghogho[3]

[1] Research Centre in Real-time and Embedded Computing Systems, Porto, Portugal
rasro@isep.ipp.pt
[2] School of Electronics and Electrical Engineering, University of Leeds, Leeds, UK
d.c.mclernon@leeds.ac.uk
[3] International University of Rabat, Rabat, Morocco
m.ghogo@leeds.ac.uk

Abstract. This paper presents a random access protocol assisted by a set of signal processing tools that significantly improve the multi-packet reception (MPR) capabilities of the system. A receiver with M antennas is mainly used to resolve collisions with multiplicity $K \leq M$. The remaining unresolved conflicts (with multiplicity $K > M$ or with decoding errors) are processed by means of protocol-induced retransmissions that create an adaptive multiple-input multiple-output (MIMO) system. This scheme, also known as NDMA (network diversity multiple access) with MPR, can achieve in ideal conditions a maximum throughput of M packets/time-slot. A further improvement is proposed here, where the receiver attempts to recover the information immediately after the reception of each (re)transmission. This is different from conventional NDMA, where this decoding process only occurs once the adaptive MIMO channel is assumed to become full-rank (i.e., once the estimated number of required retransmissions has been collected). The signals that are correctly decoded at every step of the proposed algorithm are used to mitigate interference upon the remaining contending signals by means of successive interference cancellation (SIC). The use of SIC not only improves signal reception, but most importantly reduces the required number of retransmissions to resolve a collision. Significantly high throughput figures (depending on channel/load conditions) that surpass the nominal rate ($T > M$) are reported. To the best of our knowledge this is the first random access protocol that achieves this throughput figure. Spatial and time correlation, as well as imperfections of SIC operation are also considered. In ideal conditions, the effects of SIC are found to be equivalent to a splitting tree operation. The inclusion of SIC in NDMA-MPR also opens the possibility of backwards compatibility with legacy terminals. The protocol achieves the highest throughput in the literature with minimum feedback complexity (identical to conventional NDMA). This is a significant result for future highly dense and 5G wireless networks.

© Springer International Publishing Switzerland 2015
M. Jonsson et al. (Eds.): MACOM 2015, LNCS 9305, pp. 70–86, 2015.
DOI: 10.1007/978-3-319-23440-3_5

Keywords: Retransmission diversity · Multi-packet reception · Successive interference cancellation · Cross-layer design

1   Introduction

The demand for wireless connectivity is rapidly increasing, particularly with the advent of the Internet-of-Everything (IoE), Machine-to-Machine (M2M) communications, and 5G networks. However, spectrum scarcity has reignited interest in random access or decentralized allocation to reduce signalling load and facilitate opportunistic resource sharing. Random access protocols have experienced considerable progress over the last few years. A brief review related to the topic of this paper is now given, followed by the motivation for this work and finally we outline the contributions of this paper.

1.1   Background and Previous Works

In the design of legacy random access protocols, two main assumptions were commonly used: 1) packet collisions *always* lead to the *loss* of all the transmitted information, and 2) transmissions without collision are *always correctly received*. This so called *collision model* was relatively accurate in wire-line settings. However, in wireless scenarios, it shows severe drawbacks [1]. The collision model ignores any effects of the PHY-layer, which in the case of wireless channels leads to severe inaccuracies. For example, collision-free transmissions can fail due to wireless channel fading and interference. Conversely, collisions can be resolved by signal processing or by capture effect. The ability to recover concurrent transmissions is known as multi-packet reception (MPR) [1]. The study of MPR-based random access protocols requires a new approach based on the co-design of physical (PHY) and medium access control (MAC) layers [1]-[2]. PHY-layer features need to be incorporated accurately in MAC-layer design.

The first complete MAC-PHY design was the study of ALOHA with MPR in [3], where a stochastic MPR matrix was used for throughput optimization under the assumption of a symmetrical infinite population. The extension to asymmetrical scenarios was then proposed in [4]. An extension to the case of decentralized channel state information was provided in [5], and optimization using game theory was proposed in [6]. The last few years have witnessed an intensive research using stochastic geometry for random access in multi-hop networks using signal-to-interference-plus-noise ratio (SINR) reception models (e.g., [7]).

A breakthrough in cross-layer design was the work in [8], where collisions are resolved by retransmission diversity. The algorithm was called network diversity multiple access (NDMA). In NDMA, retransmissions create an adaptive MIMO (multiple-input multiple-output) system from which collisions can be resolved via multi-user detection. Stability analysis with perfect detection/separation is given in [9] in asymmetrical settings. Stability analysis of a symmetrical NDMA-MPR protocol was later provided in [10] using imperfect collision multiplicity estimation.

1.2 Motivations and Objectives

NDMA achieves one of the highest values of throughput in wireless random access by using cross-layer concepts [8]. In NDMA, PHY-layer diversity is explicitly created by adaptive MAC retransmissions. In theory, even large collisions can be mitigated, mainly because enough diversity (retransmissions) can be adaptively created to resolve them. This means that in NDMA signals with unresolvable collisions are not discarded immediately as in ALOHA-type and SIC-based algorithms. Instead, they are stored in memory to be subsequently processed, thus leading to important capacity gains. However, there are still several issues and potential improvements on NDMA to be addressed. In the conventional *training-based* version of NDMA with M antennas at the base station (BS), the number of retransmissions is calculated based on an estimation of the collision multiplicity. If there is a collision of K users, then the BS requests $\left\lceil \frac{K}{M} \right\rceil - 1$ retransmissions from the contending users in an attempt to create a *full- rank* MIMO channel (where $\lceil \cdot \rceil$ is the ceil integer operator) [8][10]. Therefore, the maximum throughput achieved by NDMA-MPR cannot exceed M packets/time-slot. This limit is both optimistic and pessimistic at the same time. It is optimistic because multi-user detection is not perfect under finite SNR (signal-to-noise ratio) scenarios. However, it is also pessimistic because there is a chance (using appropriate decoding and a slight change in the protocol operation) that some of the collisions can be resolved with *less retransmissions* than in conventional NDMA. This opens the possibility for improvements that will be further investigated in this paper. In addition, NDMA has not been yet analysed in realistic settings with temporal and spatial correlation. This paper also addresses these issues.

1.3 Contributions and Organization

This paper proposes a significant improvement of the NDMA-MPR protocol. In this improved version, the BS attempts the decoding of the contending signals immediately after the reception of each (re)transmission. This is different from conventional NDMA, where the BS waits until the MIMO channel created by retransmissions is considered to become full-rank before processing information. In our proposed scheme, if some of the signals are correctly recovered at any stage of the algorithm, then they are used in the subsequent decoding steps and retransmissions to mitigate their interference towards the remaining signals by means of successive interference cancellation (SIC). If the remaining contending signals can not be correctly decoded, then the BS does not discard them as in other SIC-based and ALOHA-type algorithms. Instead, retransmissions are requested that will allow to process all the collected signals considering also the previously correctly decoded signals (via SIC). SIC has therefore two main functions in NDMA-MPR: improving of the probability of correct reception (as in other SIC-based algorithms), and mainly the *reduction of the number of retransmissions required to resolve a collision* (which is particular to NDMA). This leads to important gains allowing more information being correctly transmitted in a reduced number of time slots. SIC has been used in contention binary tree algorithms in [12] to also reduce the number of splitting operations (and therefore reducing the length of the contention resolution period), boosting throughput to a historical maximum (for tree algorithms) of 0.69 packets/time-slot. This paper has been inspired by the work in [12] using SIC to improve NDMA-MPR.

So, our work considers a single-hop network with symmetrical/asymmetrical features. Symmetrical settings help in visualizing the main properties of the algorithm (such as maximum stable throughput or MST), while asymmetrical settings allow for interpretation in realistic scenarios. The protocol is shown to exceed M packets/time-slot, particularly for scenarios with high traffic loads, where a large number of retransmissions enhances the effects of SIC. To the best of our knowledge, this is the first protocol to achieve this throughput figure. The combination of MPR, NDMA, and SIC shows that it is possible to achieve the highest throughput in wireless random access with a minimum expense of feedback, which is shown to be the same as the conventional NDMA. The protocol transmits more packets with a given target SINR by using less time-slots than previous solutions. In addition, the study includes correlated retransmissions, correlated antenna signals, and random phase modulation, which have not been explored before in the context of NDMA. The paper also includes the effects of imperfect SIC. In ideal conditions, the effects of SIC are shown to be equivalent to a splitting operation of packets correctly decoded. Based on our results at full traffic load, retransmissions can be also used as a resource to be allocated in the uplink of centralized networks. Furthermore, the use of SIC also opens the possibility of backwards compatibility with legacy random access. More details follow in the main body of the paper.

This paper is organized as follows. Section 2 describes the scenario and protocol operation. Section 3 presents the metrics to be studied. Section 4 addresses the calculation of the throughput region. Section 5 provides the results of simulation, and finally Section 6 draws conclusions.

2   System Model and Protocol Description

2.1   Scenario Description

Consider the wireless slotted random access network in Fig. 1 with J terminals (each one with one antenna) and one BS with M antennas. The channel between user j and the mth antenna of the BS is denoted by $h_{j,m}$. All channels are assumed to be non-dispersive and Rayleigh distributed: $h_{j,m} \sim \mathcal{CN}(0, \sigma_j^2)$. Note that users are explicitly assumed as statistically different (asymmetrical). Results will be obtained for symmetrical settings as a particular case, and for asymmetrical settings as general case. Channels will be correlated in time and space: $E[h_{j,m}^*(n)h_{j,\tilde{m}}(\tilde{n})] = \rho_{m,\tilde{m}}^{(n,\tilde{n})}\sigma_j^2$, where $(\cdot)^*$ is the complex conjugate operator and $\rho_{m,\tilde{m}}^{(n,\tilde{n})}$ is the correlation coefficient between the signal of antenna m in

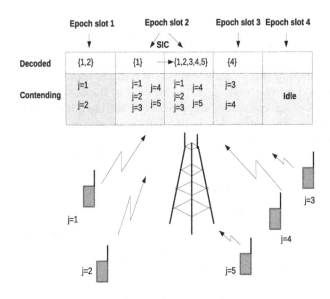

Fig. 1. System model

time slot n with the signal of antenna $\tilde{m}$ in time slot $\tilde{n}$. All channels will be generated using the following linear correlation model:

$$h_{j,m}(n) = \sqrt{R - \sum_{(\tilde{m},\tilde{n}) \neq (m,n)} \rho_{m,\tilde{m}}^{(n,\tilde{n})} Y_{j,m,n}}$$

$$+ \sum_{(\tilde{m},\tilde{n}) \neq (m,n)} \sqrt{\rho_{m,\tilde{m}}^{(n,\tilde{n})} Z_{j,n,\tilde{n}}^{(m,\tilde{m})}}, \qquad Z_{j,n,\tilde{n}}^{(m,\tilde{m})} = Z_{j,\tilde{n},n}^{(\tilde{m},m)}, \qquad (1)$$

where the variables $Y_{j,m,n}$ and $Z_{j,n,\tilde{n}}^{(m,\tilde{m})}$ are independent circular complex Gaussian random variables with zero mean and variance σ_j^2, and also $R = M \left\lceil \frac{K}{M} \right\rceil - 1$. All terminals are assumed to always have a packet ready for transmission (full-queue or dominant system assumption). The packet transmission will be 0 regulated by a random Bernoulli experiment with parameter p_j, which is the transmission probability of user j. Since collisions are resolved with adaptive retransmissions, the number of time-slots used in the resolution will be described by the random variable l. The period of time used to resolve a collision will be called contention resolution period or *epoch-slot*. The example in Fig. 1 with 5 users ($J = 5$) and two antennas ($M = 2$) shows a scenario with 4 epochs, three with active transmissions and one idle (no user transmits). One of the active epochs has length of two time-slots. This means that retransmission diversity was employed to resolve the collision.

2.2   Principles of Operation

The proposed protocol exploits *spatial* and *temporal (retransmission)* diversity
to resolve collisions. Temporal diversity is adaptively created via retransmissions
according to the number of contending signals that require further processing to
be resolved. So, at the beginning of any epoch slot, the BS is assumed to know
the identity of the contending users, and therefore it has perfect knowledge of
the collision multiplicity[1] $K = |\mathcal{T}|$, where $\mathcal{T}$ denotes the set colliding users and
$|\mathcal{U}|$ represents the cardinality of any set $\mathcal{U}$. In *conventional non-blind* NDMA,
the BS requests $\left\lceil \frac{K}{M} \right\rceil - 1$ retransmissions from the contending users to improve
rank conditions of the virtual MIMO channel [10]. Once all these retransmissions
are received, then the legacy BS is assumed to attempt multi-user decoding. In
contrast to this conventional algorithm operation, in our present work *the BS
does not wait until all the estimated number of retransmissions have been collected.* Instead, the BS attempts the processing and full decoding of the information immediately after receiving each (re)transmission using a minimum mean
square error (MMSE) receiver. Since the channel matrix is in this case *rank
deficient*, then several of the contending signals are not likely to be correctly
decoded. However, there is a non-zero probability that some of the signals can
be actually correctly decoded. All these correctly decoded signals are used in
subsequent decoding steps and time-slots to cancel their interference upon the
remaining contending signals by using SIC. This scheme is repeated after the
reception of each retransmission. The algorithm attempts to recover as much
information as possible every time-slot. When it is no longer possible to decode
information, further retransmissions are requested that will create further diversity. The algorithm stops requesting retransmissions once all the contending
signals are correctly decoded or once the number of retransmissions reaches the
value estimated in conventional NDMA (i.e., $\left\lceil \frac{K}{M} \right\rceil - 1$). The BS uses an ideal
and instantaneous binary feedback flag to request retransmissions at the end of
each time-slot.

Consider now the example of Fig. 1. The first epoch experiences two contending users, both of which have been correctly decoded in one time-slot because
the BS has precisely two antennas and their decoding operation was successful.
The second epoch experiences a collision of 5 users, which in the conventional
algorithm requires $\lceil 5/2 \rceil - 1 = 2$ further retransmissions for resolution. However, note that user $j = 1$ has been correctly decoded in the first time slot of the
epoch, and thus SIC can be used to remove its interference towards the other
contending signals. The BS requests another retransmission, and this time, with
the interference created by user $j = 1$ having been removed, the remaining 4
users can be decoded with two time diversity entries and two space diversity
sources. Note that the second retransmission (which is necessary in the origi-

---

[1] Perfect collision multiplicity estimation can be closely achieved by using cooperative,
sequential and multiple antenna processing combining [11][10]. Analysis considering
the remaining errors of collision multiplicity estimation is out of the scope of this
paper. Results obtained by the authors indicate that the results hold also in the
imperfect detection case.

nal NDMA algorithm) *was no longer required*. This illustrates the gains of the algorithm: a total of 5 transmissions were correctly received in *only two time slots*, which leads to an instantaneous rate of $5/2 = 2.5$ packets/time-slot, which exceeds the value of $M = 2$ of the nominal rate of this particular system. Note that in conventional schemes powered by SIC, once channel conditions do not allow for more packets to be correctly decoded, the algorithm stops and the non decoded information is discarded. By contrast, in our scheme retransmissions enable an additional decoding step, thus serving as complement of the SIC cycle and allowing more packets to be correctly decoded without the need of discarding information. The third epoch in Fig. 1 shows a collision of two users with only one user being correctly decoded and no further retransmissions requested, as the collision multiplicity was below the BS antenna reception capability ($K < 1$). In this case, the decoding of the signal of user $j = 3$ has failed. Remaining errors are assumed to be handled by error control/correction of upper layer protocols.

2.3   Signal Model and Protocol Steps

The signal received by the mth antenna of the BS in time slot n of an epoch given a set $\mathcal{T}$ of contending users and under SIC operation can be written as:

$$\mathbf{y}_m(n) = \sum_{j \in \mathcal{T}} \check{h}_{j,m}(n)\mathbf{s}_j - \sum_{k \in \mathcal{T}_d(n)} \check{h}_{k,m}(n)\hat{\mathbf{s}}_k + \mathbf{v}_m(n), \qquad (2)$$

where $\mathbf{s}_j = [s_j^{(0)}, \ldots, s_j^{(Q-1)}]^T$ is the packet with Q QAM symbols transmitted by user j; $\hat{\mathbf{s}}_k$ is the estimated signal of user k once it has been correctly decoded in the SIC cycle (described later in this subsection); $\mathcal{T}_d(n)$ indicates the subset of contending users that has been correctly decoded up to time slot n of an epoch slot; and $\mathbf{v}_m(n) = [v_m^{(0)}, \ldots, v_m^{(Q-1)}]^T$ is the vector of zero-mean Gaussian noise with variance σ_v^2: $v_m^{(q)}(n) \sim \mathcal{CN}(0, \sigma_v^2)$. In the previous expression, $\check{h}_{k,m}(n) = e^{-i\psi_{j,n}} h_{j,m}(n)$, where $i = \sqrt{-1}$ and $\psi_{j,n}$ is the uniformly distributed random phase used to counteract the effects of time correlation[2]. The second term in (2) corresponds to the operation of subtracting the interference of users correctly decoded in the previous steps from the main received signal. Note that under perfect SIC, once some of the signals are correctly decoded, their interference disappears in subsequent time-slots (via SIC). This is similar to a splitting operation in tree algorithms. This means that a PHY tool mimics a MAC operation with reduced feedback. This type of equivalence between PHY and MAC operations commonly arises in cross-layer design problems. Considering (2), all the collected (re)transmissions create a virtual MIMO system that can be expresed as follows [8] [9]:

$$\mathbf{Y}(n) = \mathbf{A}_{\bar{d}}(n)\mathbf{S}_{\bar{d}} + \xi\mathbf{A}_d(n)\mathbf{S}_d + \mathbf{V}(n), \qquad (3)$$

---

[2] In NDMA, time correlation degrades full-rank condition of the virtual MIMO channel matrix. Random phase modulation aims to partially counteract this effect by explicitly introducing randomness in the transmitted signals at each time-slot [8].

where $\mathbf{Y}(n)$ is the array formed by all received signals across all of the Mn resources obtained from the combination of M antennas and n time-slots; $\mathbf{A}_d(n)$ and $\mathbf{A}_{\bar{d}}(n)$ denote the MIMO channels of the set of correctly decoded and not correctly decoded users, respectively; $\mathbf{S}_d$ and $\mathbf{S}_{\bar{d}}$ are the arrays of stacked packets for both sets of users; ξ is the parameter that will be used to measure different degrees of efficiency of SIC and which depends on several PHY-layer factors such as channel estimation, the SIC stage and modulation format; and finally $\mathbf{V}(n)$ is the noise. The channel matrices can be estimated using a convenient training sequence design (see [8]). In this paper we assume perfect channel estimation. The non-decoded signals can be processed at the BS using a linear decoding matrix $\mathbf{G}(n)$ given by the MMSE criterion: $\mathbf{G}(n) = (\mathbf{A}_{\bar{d}}^H(n)\mathbf{A}_{\bar{d}}(n) + \sigma_v^2\ mathbf{I}_{nM})^{-1}\mathbf{A}_{\bar{d}}^H(n)$, where $\mathbf{I}_{nM}$ is the identity matrix of order nM and $(\cdot)^H$ is the hermitian transpose operator. This operation applied to (3) leads to:

$$\hat{\mathbf{S}}_{\bar{d}}(n) = \mathbf{W}_{\bar{d}}(n)\mathbf{S}_{\bar{d}} + \xi\mathbf{W}_d(n)\mathbf{S}_d + \mathbf{G}(n)\mathbf{V}(n), \tag{4}$$

where $\mathbf{W}_d(n) = \mathbf{G}(n)\mathbf{A}_d(n)$ and $\mathbf{W}_{\bar{d}}(n) = \mathbf{G}(n)\mathbf{A}_{\bar{d}}(n)$. The signal for user j in time-slot n in (4) will experience an instantaneous SINR given by:

$$\Gamma_j(n) = \frac{|W_{\bar{d}}^{(j,j)}(n)|^2}{\eta_j(n) + |\mathbf{g}_j(n)|^2\sigma_v^2}, \tag{5}$$

where $W_{\bar{d}}^{(j,k)}(n)$ denotes the entry of matrix $\mathbf{W}_{\bar{d}}(n)$ that corresponds to the row and column of user j and user k, respectively, and $\mathbf{g}_j(n)$ is the row of matrix $\mathbf{G}(n)$ corresponding to user j. The interference term in (5) is given by:

$$\eta_j(n) = \sum_{k\neq j, k\notin \mathcal{T}_d(n)} |W_{\bar{d}}^{(j,k)}(n)|^2 + \sum_{k\in\mathcal{T}_d(n)} \xi^2|W_d^{(j,k)}(n)|^2.$$

A packet is assumed to be correctly received if the SINR exceeds a threshold β (SINR reception model). This threshold depends on the modulation format in use and the operational block error rate (BLER)[3]. Both β and ξ will be obtained via PHY-layer simulation. The decoding operation previously described is repeated every time-slot of an epoch, and it continues until there is no change in the set of decoded users or until the maximum number of retransmissions ($\lceil\frac{K}{M}\rceil - 1$) has been collected. These steps are repeated for subsequent epoch-slots. The steps of this algorithm are summarized in Table 1. Some additional advantages can be observed in the proposed algorithm. The SIC cycle decodes packets sequentially according to SINR conditions. This includes signals that are part of the initial set of users but which do not appear again, or which only appear a few random times during the resolution period. These are typical signals of terminals in

---

[3] Under the SINR reception model, the throughput represents the average information transmitted per packet with a given BLER performance. The SINR reception model is commonly used in random access to incorporate enriched PHY-layer information in protocol design. It is also used for the study of SIC in random access (e.g. [13]).

1. Generate $\mathcal{T}$ using traffic model. Start of an epoch.
2. Set $n = 1$, $\mathcal{T}_d(n) = \mathcal{R}(n) = \emptyset$.
3. **while** $n \leq \lceil \frac{K}{M} \rceil$ & $|\mathcal{T}_d(n)| < |\mathcal{T}|$ **do**
   (a) Calculate $\Gamma_j(n)$ in (5) $\forall j \in \mathcal{T}$,
   (b) $\mathcal{T}_d(n) = \{j | \Gamma_j(n) > \beta\}$
   (c) **while** $|\mathcal{T}_d(n)| > |\mathcal{R}(n)|$ **do**
       i. $\mathcal{R}(n) = \mathcal{T}_d(n)$;
       ii. Calculate $\Gamma_j(n)$ in (5) $\forall j \notin \mathcal{T}_d(n)$;
       iii. $\mathcal{T}_d(n) = \{j | \Gamma_j(n) > \beta\}$;
   end
   (d) $n = n + 1$
end

Algorithm 1. Algorithm NDMA-MPR-SIC

ALOHA or binary tree mode or interfering signals. Therefore, the algorithm could potentially incorporate legacy terminals by recovering their signals at the end or at different stages of the decoding cycle, and also automatically reject co-channel interference.

3   Performance Metrics

The conditional reception probability $q_{\mathcal{S}|\mathcal{T}}(n)$ is defined as the joint probability that all users in $\mathcal{S} \subseteq \mathcal{T}$ experience a value of SINR $\Gamma_j(n)$ in (5) above threshold β conditional on the set of contending users $\mathcal{T}$, and on the epoch length l having reached the value n:

$$q_{\mathcal{S}|\mathcal{T}}(n) = \Pr\{\cap_{j \in \mathcal{S}} \Gamma_j(n) > \beta | \mathcal{T}, l = n\}.$$

Note that this probability is conditional on the previous decoding events in the epoch slot that have lead to a realization of n time slots (i.e., the collision was not resolved in previous slots). The throughput of terminal j is defined as the ratio of the probability of correct reception over all epoch realizations (S_j) to the average length of an epoch ($E[l]$):

$$T_j = \frac{S_j}{E[l]} = \frac{\sum_{n,\mathcal{T},j \in \mathcal{T}} \Pr\{\mathcal{T}\} \Pr\{l = n | \mathcal{T}\} q_{j|\mathcal{T}}(n)}{\sum_{n,\mathcal{T}} n \Pr\{\mathcal{T}\} \Pr\{l = n | \mathcal{T}\}}, \tag{6}$$

where $\Pr\{\mathcal{T}\}$ indicates the probability of realization of the set of contending users $\mathcal{T}$, and $\Pr\{l = n | \mathcal{T}\}$ indicates the probability mass function (pmf) of the epoch length conditional on the set of colliding users $\mathcal{T}$. These terms can be expressed as:

$$\Pr\{\mathcal{T}\} = \prod_{k \in \mathcal{T}} p_k \prod_{j \notin \mathcal{T}} \bar{p}_j,$$

and

$$\Pr\{l = n | T\} = \begin{cases} q_{T|T}(n) \prod_{t=1}^{n-1} \bar{q}_{T|T}(t), & n < \lceil K/M \rceil \\ \prod_{t=1}^{n-1} \bar{q}_{T|T}(t) & n = \lceil K/M \rceil \\ 1, & K = 0, n = 1 \end{cases},$$

where $(\bar{a}) = 1 - (a)$, for any a. The last expression indicates that a retransmission is requested whenever the resolution process has failed during the current time slot. It also indicates that the resolution period ends when all the colliding users are correctly decoded or when the maximum number of (re)transmissions ($\lceil K/M \rceil$) of the original NDMA-MPR scheme have been received. All the conditional reception probabilities will obtained via PHY-layer simulation and later used in a MAC-PHY simulation/analysis, as shown later in the section of results. Consider now the vector $\mathbf{T} = [T_1, T_2, \ldots T_J]^T$ of stacked *throughput* values, and the vector $\mathbf{p} = [p_1, p_2, \ldots p_J]^T$ of transmission probabilities. The *throughput region*, is defined as the union of all achievable values $[T_1, T_2, \ldots T_J]$ over all possible transmission policies $(0 \leq p_j \leq 1)$[14]:

$$\mathcal{C}_{\tilde{T}} = \{\tilde{\mathbf{T}} | \tilde{T}_j = T_j(\mathbf{p}), 0 \leq p_j \leq 1\}. \tag{7}$$

The throughput region is one of the main metrics in the study of random access in asymmetrical settings[14].

4 Optimization

To derive the envelope of the throughput region in (7), a multi-objective optimization of the J objective functions in (6) is proposed:

$$\mathbf{p}_{opt} = \arg\max_{\mathbf{p}} \; [T_1, T_2, \ldots T_J], \qquad 0 \leq p_j \leq 1. \tag{8}$$

Since this vector optimization usually lacks a unique solution [15], the concept of *Pareto optimality* is commonly employed. A Pareto optimal solution can be loosely defined here as the point that is at least optimum for one or more of the elements of the vector objective function (see [15] for a complete definition). The multi-objective optimization problem in (8) can be transformed into a single objective optimization problem using the method of scalarization [15]:

$$\mathbf{p}_{opt} = \arg\max_{\mathbf{p}} \sum_{k=1}^{J} \mu_k T_k, \qquad 0 \leq p_j \leq 1, \tag{9}$$

where μ_k is the relative weight given to the kth objective function. Differentiating the objective function in (9) we obtain a set of equations given by $\sum_{k=1}^{J} \mu_k \frac{\partial T_k}{\partial p_j} = 0$, $k, j = 1.., J$. The solution of this set of linear equations, independent from the values of the weighting factors μ_k, can be proved, in our context, to be equivalent to setting the following Jacobian determinant to zero [16]:

$$|\mathbf{J}| = 0, \qquad 0 \leq p_j \leq 1, \tag{10}$$

where $J_{j,k} = \frac{\partial T_k}{\partial p_j}$ is the (j, k) element of the Jacobian matrix $\mathbf{J}$. The optimum transmission policy can be obtained by solving the Jacobian determinant equation in (10) using the expressions of throughput. A closed-form solution of this problem is in general difficult to obtain. This paper proposes a method that provides a solution in closed-form by considering that the desired solution is a deviation from the solution of an equivalent collision model protocol. The solution for the optimization of the throughput region of random access protocols under the collision model results in Jacobian $\tilde{\mathbf{J}}_a$ square matrices (following the lines of the derivation of the expression in (10)) that have the following property:

$$\tilde{J}_a(j, k) = \begin{cases} x_j, & k = j \\ y_j, & k \neq j \end{cases} \tag{11}$$

which means that all the elements of a row j are all the same except for the element of the main diagonal. Under this structure, the Jacobian determinant $|\tilde{\mathbf{J}}_a|$ has been proved in ([16]) to be equal to

$$|\tilde{\mathbf{J}}_a| = 1 - \sum_j \left\{ \frac{y_j}{x_j - y_j} \right\}.$$

The structure of the Jacobian matrix for the MPR cases in general does not have the same structure as in the collision model. However, the elements can be arranged in a way that is quasi-symmetrical or slightly approximate to a collision model matrix. We can then propose a complement that produces the desired quasi-symmetrical property. This can be mathematically expressed as follows:

$$\tilde{J}_a(j, k) = J_a(j, k) + \dot{J}_a(j, k),$$

where $\dot{J}_a(j, k)$ is the element of Jacobian matrix $\dot{\mathbf{J}}_a$ that complements the original Jacobian matrix $\mathbf{J}_a$ to acquire the desired symmetrical property defined in (11). The Jacobian determinant can now be obtained (using the well known co-factors formula) as the determinant of the symmetrical collision model matrix component $\tilde{\mathbf{J}}_a$ minus the deviation component that can be obtained by analysing each one of the components (co-factors) of the complement matrix $\dot{\mathbf{J}}_a$. This can be mathematically expressed as follows:

$$|\mathbf{J}_a| = |\tilde{\mathbf{J}}_a| - \sum_{j=1}^{J} (-1)^j \{ J_a(1, j)(|\tilde{\mathbf{J}}_a^{1,j}| - |\mathbf{J}_a^{1,j}|) + \dot{J}_a(1, j)|\tilde{\mathbf{J}}_a^{1,j}| \}, \tag{12}$$

where $\mathbf{B}^{k,j}$ denotes the submatrix that is formed by removing the k-th row and the jth column of matrix $\mathbf{B}$. The expression in (12) can be solved via different numerical methods to obtain the boundary of the throughput region, as shown in the next section.

5   Results

This section presents the results that show the gains of the proposed protocol. Symmetrical and asymmetrical results will be presented. Fig. 2 and Fig. 4 show the throughput versus the transmission probability ($p_j = p, \forall j$) for a symmetrical system. The results have been calculated in a scenario with $J = 16$ users experiencing an average SNR of $\frac{\sigma^2}{\sigma_v^2} = 3$ dB ($\sigma^2 = \sigma_j^2$, $\forall j$) with noise variance $\sigma_v^2 = 1$. The results were obtained using different values of spatial and temporal correlation, and using two antenna elements ($M = 2$). For simplicity, we have considered that all antennas experience the same spatial correlation between each other (ρ_s), and also all retransmissions experience the same temporal correlation (ρ_t). Note that in a realistic scenario retransmissions and antennas farther apart in time and space from each other must experience lower correlation than those being close to each other. Therefore, our assumption of symmetrical correlation represents the worst case scenario in the correlation model in (1).

The values of β, ξ and all the conditional reception probabilities of the theoretical formulae obtained in previous sections have been obtained via PHY-layer simulation with perfect channel estimation, using a packet length of $Q = 100$ BPSK symbols, and considering a packet is correctly decoded when the number of symbol errors is below $N_e = 10$. The effects of different SIC stages have also been considered when obtaining ξ. This means that packets with a given BLER contain some symbol errors that can contribute to the incorrect decoding of other packets when their signals are used to subtract interference via SIC (i.e., error propagation). The value ξ is therefore used to model the residual interference caused by the symbols containing some errors in the set of users considered as correctly decoded.

The algorithm with and without random phase modulation is tagged, respectively, NMSP and NMS. The acronyms indicate the combination of NDMA, MPR, SIC, and phase modulation. For purposes of comparison, the figure also includes the results of the conventional NDMA-MPR with and without phase modulation and for ALOHA MPR (labelled AM). The results show the high performance gains of the proposed algorithm and how random phase modulation helps to alleviate, although not completely counteract, the effects of temporal correlation in both the proposed algorithm and in the conventional NDMA-MPR (both algorithms show some improvement). We recall the reader that the random phase modulation helps in inducing full-rank conditions in scenarios with high temporal channel correlation. Spatial correlation is also shown to reduce throughput due to lack of diversity gains, particularly for ALOHA. Note that in all cases the proposed algorithm has surpassed M packets/time-slot, which means the scheme achieves, to the best of our knowledge, one of the highest values of throughput in the literature of random access. This means that the protocol exploits as much as possible the available resources, dynamically adapting to the different collision sizes by enabling retransmissions to complement the baseline multi-packet reception capabilities of the system, and using SIC to refine detection and to eliminate those retransmissions that are not necessary to resolve the collision. The algorithm also improves access delay and energy consumption, mainly because the use of SIC reduces the average number of time-slots required to resolve a collision.

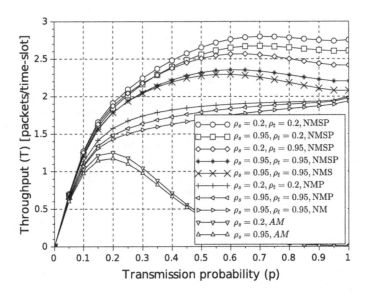

Fig. 2. Throughput T vs. Tx. probability p using $M = 2$, and $\frac{\sigma_j^2}{\sigma_v^2} = 3$dB, with real uncoded packets, parameterised on ρ_s, ρ_t and algorithm type (NMSP, NMS, NM and AM). Note that $p = p_j \ \forall j$.

It can be observed that at full traffic load ($p \to 1$), the gains of the algorithm become particularly attractive. At full load the algorithm resembles a centralized resource allocation problem, where retransmissions can be used for resource allocation in the time domain. This means that in centralized uplink systems users can be scheduled to share the exact same transmission resource over different time-slots, mimicking a collision that can be resolved via the proposed algorithm combining multiple antennas, retransmissions and SIC.

Fig. 3 shows results using realistic uncoded packets with BPSK modulation and with $Q = 100$ symbols. The SINR model is not used in this case. All packets are generated and processed according to the description of the algorithm. All the other settings are identical to the settings used in Fig. 2. The results prove that the algorithm performs very similar to the case studied in Fig. 2 with a performance that exceeds the barrier of M packets/time-slot. It can be observed in both cases that at full traffic load, the gains of the algorithm are particularly attractive.

In the previous two figures, we have assumed imperfect SIC operation. This means that remaining symbol errors in some of the packets considered as correctly decoded can cause error propagation when using SIC. The results in Fig. 4 assume perfect operation of SIC. The objective is to assess the potential gains of SIC. All the simulation settings are identical to the previous two cases, except for the value of ξ, which in this case was set deliberately to zero ($\xi = 0$). We can observe in the results that the gains can double the nominal rate of the system ($T > 4$), which is a significant result. This opens the possibility of designing an appropriate modulation and coding scheme that can achieve nearly

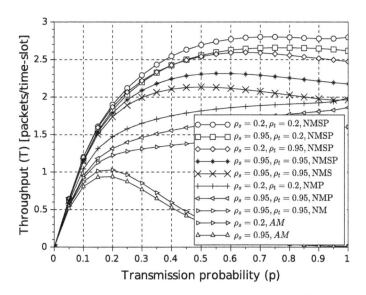

Fig. 3. Throughput T vs. Tx. probability p using $M = 2$, and $\frac{\sigma_j^2}{\sigma_v^2} = 3$dB, with real uncoded packets, parameterised on ρ_s, ρ_t and algorithm type (NMSP, NMS, NM and AM). Note that $p = p_j \ \forall j$.

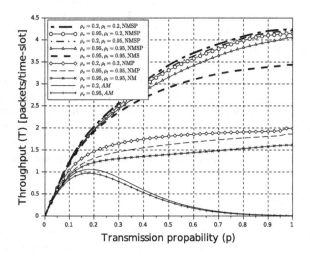

Fig. 4. Throughput T vs. Tx. probability p using $M = 2$, and $\frac{\sigma_j^2}{\sigma_v^2} = 3$dB, with real uncoded packets, parameterised on ρ_s, ρ_t and algorithm type (NMSP, NMS, NM and AM). Note that $p = p_j \ \forall j$.

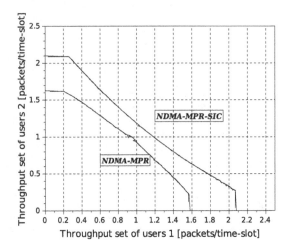

Fig. 5. Throughput region for a system with two subsets of users, $J_1 = J_2 = 8$, with SNRs of 3 dB and 5dB, respectively

perfect SIC and thus boost throughput figures close to the upper limit shown in Fig. 4.

Fig. 5 shows the throughput region for a system with two subsets of users, with J_1 and J_2 users each, where $J_1 = J_2 = 8$. A Newton-Raphson algorithm was used to solve (12) for different values of transmission probabilities and then obtain the boundary of the throughput region, which is also the Pareto frontier of the optimization problem in (8). The average SNR of both sets is set to 3 dB and 5 dB, respectively, with all other settings identical to the previous cases. The outer curve represents the boundary of the NDMA-MPR-SIC protocol, whereas the inner curve represents the NDMA-MPR protocol. SIC enlarges the throughput region exceeding (in most of the cases) the nominal rate of M packets/time slot. An enlarged throughput regions brings several benefits to a random access protocol, not only in terms of individual capacity figures, but also in the design of low-complex linear resource allocation policies within the boundaries of the region. It has been also proved in previous works (i.e., [14]), that convex throughput regions allow protocols also to achieve a better trade-off between different metrics such as fairness, power consumption, and sum-throughput.

6   Conclusions

This paper has presented a significant improvement over the NDMA-MPR protocol by using SIC. Unlike the conventional protocol, the proposed scheme allows the BS to attempt the decoding of the colliding signals immediately after the reception of each (re)transmission, rather than waiting until the created (virtual) MIMO channel is assumed to become full-rank. If some of the signals are correctly decoded, then an additional decoding cycle based on SIC is used to improve reception of the remaining signals and to also reduce the number of retransmissions required in the original algorithm. The result is a protocol that: (i) considerably improves the performance of previous algorithms using minimum feedback complexity (highest throughput in literature); (ii) is potentially backwards compatible with legacy random access, and (iii) that is also a potential solution for centralized systems. Finally, the extension to semi-centralized and multi-hop systems using stochastic geometry and imperfect collision multiplicity detection is an attractive future research topic that is currently under progress.

References

1. Dimic, G., Sidiropoulos, N.D., Zhang, R.: Medium access control-physical cross-layer design. IEEE Sig. Proc. Mag. **21**(5), 40–50 (2004)
2. Srivastaya, V., Montani, M.: Cross-layer design: a survey and the road ahead. IEEE Commun. Mag. **43**(12), 112–119 (2005)
3. Ghez, S., Verdu, S., Schwartz, S.: Stability properties of slotted Aloha with multipacket reception capability. IEEE Transactions on Automatic Control **33**(7), 640–649 (1988)
4. Naware, V., Mergen, G., Tong, L.: Stability and delay of finite-user slotted ALOHA with multipacket reception. IEEE Transactions on Information Theory **51**(7), 2636–2656 (2005)
5. Ngo, M.H., Krishnamurthy, V., Tong, L.: Optimal hannel-Aware ALOHA Protocol for random access in WLANs with multipacket reception and decentralized CSI. IEEE Trans. on Sig. Processing **56**(6), 2575–2588 (2008)
6. Ngo, M.H., Krishnamurty, V.: Game theoretic cross-layer transmission policies in multipacket reception wireless networks. IEEE Trans. on Sig. Proc. **55**(5), 1911–1926 (2007)
7. Hanawal, M.K., Altman, E., Baccelli, F.: Stochastic geometry based medium access games in wireless Ad Hoc networks. IEEE Journal on Selected Areas in Comm. **30**(11), 2146–2157 (2012)
8. Tsatsanis, M.K., Zhang, R., Banerjee, S.: Network-assisted diversity for random access wireless networks. IEEE Transactions on Sig. Proc. **48**(3), 702–711 (2000)
9. Dimic, G., Sidiropoulos, N.D., Tassiulas, L.: Wireless networks with retransmission diversity access mechanisms: stable throughput and delay properties. IEEE Trans. on Sig. Proc. **51**(8), 2019–2030 (2003)
10. Samano-Robles, R., Gameiro, A.: Stability properties of network diversity multiple access protocols with multiple antenna reception and imperfect collision multiplicity estimation. Journal of Computer Networks and Commun. **2013**, Article ID. 984956, 10 pages
11. Samano-Robles, R., Ghogho, M., McLernon, D.C.: Cooperative and sequential user detection for wireless network diversity multiple access protocols. In: 3rd Int. Symposium on Wireless Per. Comp., ISWPC 2008, pp. 189–193, May 2008
12. Yingqun, Y., Giannakis, G.B.: High-throughput random access using successive interference cancellation in a tree algorithm. IEEE Transactions on Info.Theory **53**(12), 4628–4639 (2007)

13. Mollanoori, M., Ghaderi, M.: On the performance of successive interference cancellation in random access networks. In: IEEE CS Conference on Sensor, Mesh and Ad Hoc Communications and Networks (SECON), pp. 461–469, June 2012
14. Luo, J., Ephremides, A.: On the throughput, capacity, and stability regions of random multiple access. IEEE Trans. on Info. Theory **52**(6), 2593–2607 (2006)
15. Boyd, S., Vandenberghe, L.: Convex optimization. Cambridge University Press (2004)
16. Samano-Robles, R., Ghogho, M., McLernon, D.C.: Wireless networks with retransmission diversity and carrier sense multiple access. IEEE Transactions on Sig. Proc. **57**(9), 3722–3726 (2009)

Information Theory

Distortion Avoidance While Streaming Public Safety Video in Smart Cities

Evgeny Khorov$^{(\boxtimes)}$, Andrey Gushchin, and Alexander Safonov

Network Protocols Research Lab,
Institute for Information Transmission Problems, Moscow, Russia
{khorov,guschin,safa}@iitp.ru

Abstract. The need for anytime, anywhere access to information has extended from the general public to the public safety community. The ever increasing demand for mission critical services includes streaming video (surveillance, remote monitoring, etc.). In the paper, we address the issue of transmission of protected video stream in the presence of sporadic queue overflows occurring due to dynamic video content and highly varying wireless channel condition.

1 Introduction

The need for anytime, anywhere access to information has extended from the general public to the public safety community. The ever increasing demand for mission critical services includes streaming of real time video (surveillance, remote monitoring, etc.) [1–3]. Up to date video content compression techniques make the bitrate of data streams carrying such content variable and their structure extremely complex. The importance of a stream packet, i.e. the effect of the packet loss to the perceptual quality at the receiver (viewer) side, varies in a huge range.

Even with channel resource supply [4,5] and advanced coding techniques [6,7], from time to time the transmitter may find lack of capacity to deliver all packets in time due to variable stream bitrate and network conditions. In such a case, the packets with the exceeded delay bound are dropped. To minimize the perceptual video quality degradation, some structure-aware methods, e.g. I-frame delay (IFD) [8], determine the type and importance of each frame and drop the least important frames.

The question is what could be done in public safety networks, when the video content is encrypted so that the frame type is concealed. In the paper, we address this question and study the efficiency of an easy implementation method to detect packets of the lowest priority. For that, we develop a solid methodology to evaluate the amount of errors occurring when streaming protected video in the presence of sporadic queue overflows and compare various frame dropping strategies. This methodology is another contribution of this paper.

The rest of the paper is organized as follows. In Section 2, we give a short background on MPEG-4 video structure and the IFD algorithm, while

M. Jonsson et al. (Eds.): MACOM 2015, LNCS 9305, pp. 89–100, 2015.
DOI: 10.1007/978-3-319-23440-3_7

Section 2.3 provides a brief overview of the considered in the public safety communication system, which streams video. In Section 3, preliminary statistical analysis of a set of video samples is given. Also in this Section, we show how to adopt IFD for public safety video. In Section 4, we describe the methodology to evaluate the performance of the considered solution in the presence of sporadic queue overflows when transmitting video samples over wireless channel. Also in this Section, we obtain numerical results. Section 5 concludes the paper.

2   Background and Problem Statement

2.1   MPEG-4 Background

In this paper, we focus on the MPEG-4 technology which — together with similar H.264 — has already become the predominant standard for providing digital video services. An MPEG-4 video stream may contain frames of various types: intra-coded (I-frame), predictive-coded (P-frame) and bidirectionally-coded (B-frame). The I-frame contains information about the whole video frame. A sequence of frames between two consequential I-frames is called Group of Pictures (GoP). The P-frame contains only information about the difference between coded video frame and previous reference frame which can be either a P-frame or an I-frame. The B-frame is coded using information from both previous and following reference frames. Such a complex scheme provides high compression, since P-frames are typically (but not always!) smaller then I-frames, and B-frames are typically smaller than I-frames [9].

When a video is streamed over a network, packets of the stream impact the perceptual video quality differently [10]. If packets carrying a B-frame are dropped, the perceptual video quality remains close to ideal, since no other frames depend on B-frames. If a P-frame or an I-frame is corrupted or lost, all dependent frames, i.e. up to the end of the GoP, face decoding errors, so the video quality degrades dramatically [11]. Hence, I-frames are the most important for decoding process, as all other frames in GoPs depend on their information. P-frames are less important than I-frames, while B-frames are the least important.

On the one hand, the described coding scheme ensures high compression of the video, but on the other hand, it makes the size of consequent frames significantly different from each other. Together with variable network conditions, stream bit rate peaks may make it impossible to deliver video packets in time, which cause packet losses and perceptual video quality degradation. To limit video quality degradation, some methods anticipate such situations by limiting the queue size, and drop packets carrying the least important frames first when the queue overflows.

2.2   I-Frame Delay

Proposed in [8], the I-frame delay (IFD) implements such an approach. It assigns priority to each packet by the type of the frame it contains. IFD drops all packets carrying the least important frames until the overflow is eliminated. Comparing two frames of the same type, the newer one is considered to be more important. Comparing two frames of various types, B-frames are the least important, while I-frames are the most important. Moreover, I-frames shall be never dropped. Even if the delay bound is crossed for an I-frame and the frame is not displayed itself, it is used to decode following P- and B-frames until the next I-frame in the stream appears.

To determine frame types, IFD performs deep packet inspection to find unique hexadecimal sequence 00:00:01:B6:XY, which starts a new video frame according to the MPEG-4 standard. The first two bits of X say its type.

2.3   Public Safety Communication System

Due to security reasons, video content transmitted over public safety networks may be encrypted. Considered in the paper communication systems encapsulate video into MPEG-TS (MPEG Transport Stream), which is transmitted via the RTP/UDP/IP/... protocol stack.

MPEG Transport Stream (MPEG-TS) splits MPEG-4 binary stream into fixed-sized TS packets. Each new video frame starts a new TS packet, while the old one is filled with the stuffing bits. TS packets containing the video stream are mixed with those carrying audio, subtitles if any, service and other relevant information. Video packets can be found in a multiplexed stream by the PID (Program ID) value in the headers. Analyzing the body of TS packets which belong to a plain video stream and looking for sequence 00:00:01:B6, one can find the structure of the video stream. However, the body of TS packets carrying public safety video is encrypted and frame types are concealed, while all headers remain open.

Fortunately, in addition to the PID field, the headers of TS packets may contain a mark, which identifies the beginning of new video frame, so that all TS packets between two consequent packets with the mark contain information about the same video frame. It means that MPEG-TS headers help to determine frame borders, but not its type.

To our best knowledge, no IFD-like algorithm deals with such a case. Being designed for video streams with open structure, IFD-like algorithms are not applicable to video streams with concealed structure sent in considered scenarios. Several papers (e.g. [12]) suggest to drop the longest packet in such a situation, since their drop release much channel time. On the other, since B-frames are typically (but not always!) the smallest frames in the video [9], one can perform dropping the smallest frames.

The goal of this paper is to study how B-frames can be identified in the public safety video stream, and to study the efficiency of the proposed approach.

3 Preliminary Statistical Analysis of the MPEG-4 Streams

3.1 Hypothesis

To develop a method to find B-frames in an encrypted video stream, let us pay attention to the following feature of the MPEG-4 compressing technique. By design, a video frame encoded as I-frame requires more bits than the same frame encoded as P-frame. Similarly, encoding as P-frame results in larger frame than encoding as B-frame [9]. Assuming consecutive frames in a video stream changes just a little, in any sequence of frames, B-frames are typically smaller than P- and I-frames.

However, this statement may be false, as compression ratio for different frames varies a lot due to the nature of the video content. For example, when the scene changes and a new GoP starts, the I-frame and following P-frames may appear to be smaller than B-frames of the previous GoP.

Let us call "w-window" a sequence of w frames in a video stream and consider the following hypothesis. **A frame arbitrarily chosen out of $k \leq w$ smallest frames in a w-window is a B-frame.** Calculating the probability that the hypothesis holds is equivalent to calculating the probability to drop B-frames when dropping k smallest frames in the queue. Note, that we consider frame dropping only when the queue is long enough, and do not consider advance frame dropping, since it is not worth [13].

3.2 Video Samples Database

To test the hypothesis, we need a relevant video sample database. As it is shown in [14], video streams can be classified into several groups depending on their content and amount of motion. For example, in a newscast the image usually changes slightly: a person seating and reading the news on a static background. Even if some parts of such a video stream are lost, the image corruption is usually negligible for a viewer. The football match is dynamic and contains a lot of moving objects, so any loss of data leads to noticeable and annoying image corruption. Many papers consider the following types of videos: "football" which is dynamic, "news" which is almost static, and "movie" containing different scenes. Video samples typical for public safety networks can also be mapped to these types.

To obtain statistically meaningful results, we create a video database with 9 samples of these types. For "movie" we choose the three top rating movies according to the Internet Movie Database [16]. For "football" we choose three football matches of Euro 2012. For "news" we consider three records of different TV talk shows and newscasts.

All the samples are coded using avidemux software [17] and Divx video codec [18] with the following parameters. Frame rate is 25 fps. The number of B-frames per P-frame equals 2. GoP structure is adaptive: number of frames between two sequential I-frames are chosen adaptively by the codec based on the video content. Maximum GoP size equals 300.

3.3   Experiment

To test the proposed hypothesis, we run the following experiment with each sample. Consider a window of w frames sliding frame-by-frame from the beginning to the end of the video sample. At every step i, we calculate $p_i = \frac{b_i}{k}$, where b_i equals the number of B-frames out of k *smallest* frames within window. By averaging over $\langle p_i \rangle_i$, we obtain the probability that an arbitrary chosen frame out of k smallest frames is a B-frame.

3.4   Numerical Results

For each $w = \{3, 5, 10\}$ corresponding to 120 ms, 200 ms and 400 ms respectively for a 25 fps sample, we vary $k \in \{\overline{1, w}\}$ in a series of experiments described above. After that, we average the results over all samples of same type.

Fig. 1 shows the probability that, for given w and k, the hypothesis holds. It proves that the hypothesis holds in more than 99% of cases for $k < w/2$. Note that the $k = w$ points indicate the percentage of B-frames in video samples.

Having tested the proposed hypothesis, let us study how the errors are located along the video sample, i.e. when we drop I- or P-frames instead of B-frames. For that, we average p_i not over the whole video sample but in window W: $\langle p_i \rangle_t^{t+W-1}$, where $W = 1000$. Fig. 2 shows such a distribution for "news" for $w = 10$ and $k = 5$. The peaks at 00:27, 00:56 and 01:23 are caused by the structure of the video stream. To improve compression, the codec does not use B-frames for some time. For example at 01:23 the structure of the video stream looks like IPPBPPPPPP. Outside the peaks the hypothesis holds with probability close to 100%.

As the result of the described analysis, we propose a simple modification of the IFD algorithm, which selects the shortest frame, when it needs to drop a frame. Further we refer to it as the SFB (the smallest frame is a B-frame) method.

4   Performance Evaluation of SFB in a Network Scenario

The results obtained in Section 3 show that SFB may make mistakes and drop P- or I-frames instead of B-frames. In this Section, we study *how such mistakes affect video quality in public safety networks*.

Considered the same video samples as in Section 3.2, we compare the following approaches to drop a frame from the queue (further refereed to as filters).

- SFB described in Section 3.4.
- The Ideal filter, which knows the type of each frame, i.e. IFD for the video with known structure.
- The Random filter, which randomly choose a frame from the queue and return it as a B-frame[1].

---

[1] In addition to these methods, we have also considered ones which drops the head or the tail frame, however they provide results very similar to the Random method. So we exclude them from the further description.

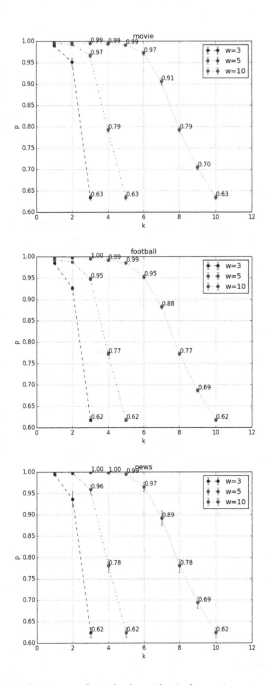

Fig. 1. Probability to confirm the hypothesis for various types of samples

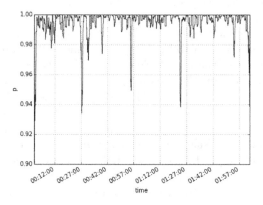

Fig. 2. Distribution of $\langle p_i \rangle_t^{t+W-1}$ over time for "news"

4.1   Methodology

To perform fair comparison, we need to obtain statistically meaningful results. It means that we shall transmit thousands hours of video in the same (determined, fixed) conditions, which is hardly possible with real equipment. For these reasons, we develop a simulation model. Let us describe it in detail.

First of all, we shall note that similar to Section 3 in our model we deal with video frames, not network packets. It means that we assume that the frames are enqueued as the whole, and to drop a piece of information, we drop the whole frame. The model time unit τ is the interframe interval.

The events which cause delay bound violation and the methods to predict such event are out of the scope of the paper. What we consider is just sometimes queue overflows and a piece of information shall be dropped from the queue. In these moments, the number of frames in the queue is $w = \lfloor \frac{D}{\tau} \rfloor$, where D is frames delay bound.

The number of overflows in a time unit has Poisson distribution with parameter $\lambda = \frac{1}{avg\_shift}$, where avg_shift is the average distance in frames between two consequent overflows. So we determine the series of overflow moments $\{t_i\}$ which are the same for all filters.

If each overflow causes the drop of a single frame, one may note that SFB outperforms the Random filter just because SFB removes less information. To avoid such an unjust accusation and to make the comparison fair, we need filters remove the same amount of information. For that, we define step function $S(k\tau)$ which is the number of bytes to be removed from the video stream from the beginning of the video stream till moment $k\tau$. Removing frames from the queue shall continue until total number $R(k\tau)$ of removed bytes exceed $S(k\tau)$. If $S(k\tau) < R(k\tau)$, i.e. the amount of already removed data is enough to avoid overflow, IFD shall not be applied. Given K, the total number of frames in the stream, we can state that values $R^{filter}(K\tau)$ for various filters are almost the same, i.e. the absolute discrepancy does not exceed maximum frame size, while the relative discrepancy decreases with the number of overflows.

The amount of information to be dropped in time unit τ cannot exceed the amount of information in the queue. Since the size of video frames varies, we define that each overflow which occurs at $t_i \in [k\tau, (k+1)\tau)]$ increases $S(k\tau)$ by the average frame size in window w backward from frame k, which is the head frame in the queue at moment $k\tau$.

To summarize, we select moments t_i when overflows occur, then we set amount $S(t_i)$ of data that shall be dropped from the queue to eliminate the overflow, and then we apply filters in selected moments t_i such that the total amount of dropped data does not exceed $S(t_i)$

To obtain statistically meaningful results, we generate $N = 10$ series t_i and $S(t_i)$ for each video sample.

4.2   Video Quality Metric

To estimate the quality of video samples with dropped frames, we use the Mean Square Error (MSE) metric [15] which compares video samples frame by frame. For a pair of frames, the MSE value is calculated as follows:

$$MSE_n = \frac{1}{WH} \sum_{w=1}^{W} \sum_{h=1}^{H} |I_o^n(w,h) - I_r^n(w,h)|^2,$$

where $I_o^n(w,h)$ and $I_r^n(w,h)$ are the luminance components of the pixel with coordinates (w,h) of the original (o) and received (r) video frames, respectively, W and H are the width and the height of the image in pixels. The MSE value for the whole video fragment is the sum of MSE values of all its frames. Dropped frames have no impact on the MSE values, which is reasonable since the viewer can hardly notice that the interframe interval has doubled. However, the losses of I- and P-frames corrupt dependent frames which increase MSE for them.

4.3   Performance Evaluation

We conduct a series of experiments and average the MSE values for each video sample. Although the results look quiet similarly for the videos of the same type, the MSE values differ because of various luminance of them.

Fig. 3 shows the results of comparison of various filters obtained for "movie" transmitted under different conditions. In all the considered scenarios, SFB provides the same video quality as the Ideal filter, while the Random filter gives significantly higher MSE values. When the overflows are rare and w is high enough ($w \geq 5$), both the Ideal and the SFB filter typically do not drop P-frames and thus provide the MSE value close to zero. With smaller w and frequent overflows, the queue does not contain enough B-frames to be removed and the MSE value increases. When overflows occur too often, the SFB filter may provide worse

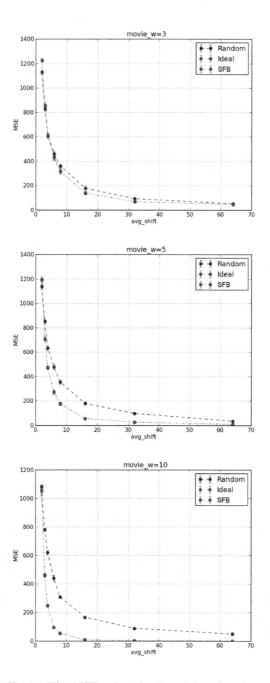

Fig. 3. The MSE values for "movie" and various w

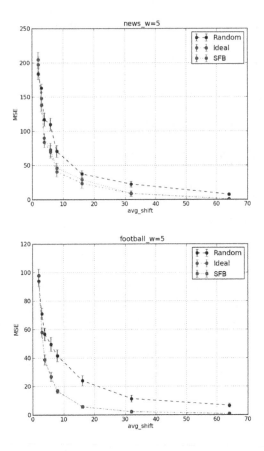

Fig. 4. The MSE values for various types of samples

efficiency than even the Random one, since it drops much more frames. However this situation can hardly be considered as a scenario of interest, since the MSE value is extremely high (and similar) for all the filters, and the perceptual video quality is unacceptable. Since the Random filter randomly drops frames, its efficiency hardly depends on w.

Finally let us show some results obtained with the samples of the other types, see Fig. 4. Although the figures differ, the behavior for the filters is similar to the described above.

5   Conclusion

Streaming of compressed video is tricky as not all packets are of equal value. It is even more tricky when the stream is previously encrypted, so that stream structure is concealed. When the queue overflows, something has to be dropped, and the question is which packets are the minimal loss for the perceptual quality. This paper study an easy implementation strategy to drop the smallest (in bytes) video frame whenever queue overflows. For that, we develop the solid methodology to evaluate the amount of errors occurring when the strategy is applied for a set of real video samples.

Acknowledgments. The reported study was carried out in IITP RAS and supported by Russian Science Foundation, agreement No 14-50-00150 (preliminary statistical analysis in Section 3), and RFBR, research project No. 14-07-31233 mol_a (performance evaluation of SFB with video quality metric in Section 4).

Some results of the work were obtained using computational resources of MCC NRC "Kurchatov Institute" (http://computing.kiae.ru/).

References

1. Interoperable Mission Critical Broadband/Narrowband Solution for Public Safety Communications in creating the Shared Wireless Broadband Network. EADS and Alcatel-Lucent Strategic White Paper (2011). http://www.cassidiancommunications.com/pdf/WhitePaper_AL_EADS.pdf
2. Bellalta, B., et al.: Performance evaluation of IEEE 802.11 p-enabled vehicular video surveillance system. IEEE Communications Letters **18**(4), 708–711
3. Belyaev, E., et al.: Robust vehicle-to-infrastructure video transmission for road surveillance applications. IEEE Transactions on Vehicular Technology
4. Ivanov, A.S., Lyakhov, A.I., Khorov, E.M.: Analytical Model of Batch Flow Multihop Transmission in Wireless Networks with Channel Reservations. Automation and Remote Control **76**(7) (2015)
5. Kiryanov, A.G., Loginov, V.A., Lyakhov, A.I., Khorov, E.M.: Analytical model of P-persistent queue management method for multimedia streaming over wireless networks. Journal of Communications Technology and Electronics **60**(12) (2015). ISSN 10642269
6. Frolov, A.: An upper bound on the minimum distance of LDPC codes over GF(q). In: IEEE International Symposium on Information Theory, June 14–19, 2015
7. Zhilin, I., Rybin, P., Zyablov, V.: High-rate codes for high-reliability data transmission. In: IEEE International Symposium on Information Theory, June 14–19, 2015
8. Burza, M., Kang, J., van der Stok, P.: Adaptive Streaming of MPEG-based Audio/Video Content over Wireless Networks. Journal of Multimedia **2**(2) (April 2007). ISSN 17962048
9. Isovic, D., Fohle, G.: Analysis of MPEG-2 Video Streams (2002). https://www.researchgate.net/publication/2532958_Analysis_of_MPEG-2_Video_Streams
10. Greengrass, J., Evans, J., Begen, A.C.: Not All Packets Are Equal, Part I: Streaming Video Coding and SLA Requirements. IEEE Internet Computing **13**(1), 70–75 (2009)
11. Greengrass, J., Evans, J., Begen, A.C.: Not all packets are equal, part 2: The impact of network packet loss on video quality. IEEE Internet Computing **13**(2), 74–82 (2009)
12. Dimitriou, S., et al.: A new service differentiation scheme: size based treatment. In: 2008 IEEE International Conference on Telecommunications, Piscataway, NJ, USA, June 16, 2008

13. Bankov, D., Khorov, E., Lyakhov, A.: Is it worth to predict overflows during video streaming over wireless networks? In: Proc. of IEEE BlackSeaCom, May 2015
14. Ries, M., de Arriba, C.C., Nemethova, O., Rupp, M.: Content based video quality estimation for H.264/AVC video streaming. In: Proc. Proceedings of IEEE Wireless and Communications & Networking Conference, Hong Kong, March 2007
15. Bankov, D., Khorov, E., Lyakhov, A.: Fast quality assessment of videos transmitted over lossy networks. MSE calculation for video streaming in lossy networks. In: Proc. IEEE International conference Engineering & Telecommunications - En&T 2014, Moscow, Russia (2014)
16. Internet Movie Database. http://www.imdb.com/
17. Avidemux video editor. http://www.avidemux.org/
18. Divx Video codec. http://www.divx.com/en/software/video-codec

On the Channel Capacity of an Order Statistics-Based Single-User Reception in a Multiple Access System

Dmitry Osipov[1,2(✉)]

[1] Institute for Information Transmission Problems,
Russian Academy of Sciences, 19 Bolshoy Karetny Lane, Moscow 127994, Russia
d_osipov@iitp.ru
[2] National Research University Higher School of Economics,
20 Myasnitskaya Ulitsa, Moscow 101000, Russia

Abstract. In what follows an order-statistics based single user reception in a communication system operating under multiuser interference is considered. This paper deals with the problem of finding channel capacity of the channel corresponding to the system under consideration.

Keywords: Multiuser interference · Order statistics · Single user receiver · Capacity

1   Introduction

Interference is one of the main factors limiting the performance of the modern communication systems. Previously a number of channel models were introduced in order to investigate the effect of multiuser interference (see e.g. [1–3]) or jamming (see e.g.[7]) on the channel capacity. In case of severe interference however robust reception techniques are required since traditional decision statistics turn out to be ineffective. Recently a number of robust order-statistics based detectors were proposed [4–6]. Hereinafter a single user receiver operating under interference and employing a low complexity order-statistics based reception technique proposed in [6] will be considered.

2   Channel Model

Let us consider the following channel model: the input of the channel is a length q binary vector of Hamming weight 1 and the corresponding output is a length q binary vector of Hamming weight α. Let us designate the input vector corresponding to a certain time instant as $\bar{X}_s$ and the corresponding output vector as

The reported study was supported by the RFBR, research project No. 14-07-31197 mol_a.

M. Jonsson et al. (Eds.): MACOM 2015, LNCS 9305, pp. 101–107, 2015.
DOI: 10.1007/978-3-319-23440-3_8

$\bar{Y}_s$. In what follows we shall assume that with probability p the vector $\bar{Y}_s$ covers $\bar{X}_s$ i.e.

$$\bar{X}_s \wedge \bar{Y}_s = \bar{X}_s \qquad (1)$$

where $\wedge$ designates element wise conjunction. Correspondingly with probability $\tilde{p} = 1 - p$

$$\bar{X}_s \wedge \bar{Y}_s = \bar{0} \qquad (2)$$

Furthermore we shall assume that all the output vectors meeting the condition (1) are equiprobable and the same holds for the output vectors meeting the condition (2).

Let us now consider a real-life communication system that can be described by the channel model under consideration. We assume that a user is transmitting information via a channel split into Q identical nonoverlapping subchannels. These subchannels can be allocated either in the time domain (in this case each subchannnel can be e.g. a time slot with a certain number in a TH-IR-UWB system employing PPM [8,9]) or in the frequency domain (in this case each subchannel can be e.g. a subcarrier in a system employing OFDM [10]).

In what follows it will be assumed that the user under consideration transmits $q - ary$ symbols. Whenever a user is to transmit a $q - ary$ symbol it places 1 in the position of the vector $\bar{x}_g$ corresponding to the symbol in question within the scope of the mapping in use (in what follows it will be assumed that all the positions of the vector are enumerated from 1 to Q, moreover for the sake of simplicity (but without loss of generality) we shall assume that the 1st subchannel corresponds to 0, the 2nd subchannel corresponds to 1 and so on. Thus it will be assumed that each vector $\bar{x}_g$ can be represented as $\bar{x}_g = \begin{bmatrix} \bar{X}_g \\ \bar{Z} \end{bmatrix}$ where $\bar{X}_g$ is the length q vector with one non-zero entry corresponding to the symbol under consideration, and $\bar{Z}$ is an all-zero vector of length $Q-q$). Then a random permutation of the aforesaid vector is performed and the resulting vector $\bar{\chi}_g = \pi_g (\bar{x}_g)$ is sent via the channel in use (permutations are selected equiprobably from the set of all possible permutations and the choice is performed whenever a symbol is to be transmitted); i.e. a signal is sent via the subchannel corresponding to the only non-zero entry of the vector $\bar{\chi}_g$. Hereinafter it will be assumed that K interfering signals are transmitted via the channel in use throughout the period of time within which the user under consideration transmits. This model can be used to describe a multiple access system where all the users transmit using the same method that has been described above (uncoordinated transmission in a multiple access system) or a communication system that is jammed by another communication system operating in the same channel (if the subchannels via which the interfering signals are transmitted are chosen without replacement since different interfering users can choose the same sunchannels) or a communication system under intentional jamming (if the subchannels via which the interfering signals are transmitted are chosen with replacement since the jammer can transmit jamming signals via different subchannels.)

Note that the receiver is assumed to be synchronized with the transmitter of the user. Therefore all the permutations done within the scope of transmission of the codeword in question are known to the user. The receiver measures energies at the outputs of all subchannels (let us designate the vector of the measurements as $\bar{\varpi}_g$ where g is the number of the transmitted vector) and applies inverse permutation to each vector $\bar{\varpi}_g$ corresponding to the respective vector thus reconstructing the initial order of elements and obtaining vector $\bar{w}_g = \pi_g^{-1}(\bar{\varpi}_g)$ where each vector $\bar{w}_g$ can be represented in the following form $\bar{w}_g = \begin{bmatrix} \bar{\omega}_g \\ \bar{\theta}_g \end{bmatrix}$, where $\bar{\omega}_g$ is a length q column vector and $\bar{\theta}_g$ is a length $Q - q$ column vector. Let us consider a matrix $W = [\bar{w}_1, \bar{w}_2, \ldots, \bar{w}_n]$ and the submatrix $\Omega = [\bar{\omega}_1, \bar{\omega}_2, \ldots, \bar{\omega}_n]$ (that is the submatrix corresponding to the q first rows of the matrix W). Please note that the matrix Ω contains all the information about the codeword sent by the user under consideration. Let us assume that for any vector $\bar{\omega}_i$ there is a corresponding vector $\tilde{\omega}_i$ obtained by sorting the elements of the vector $\bar{\omega}_i$ in the descending order. For any given value of the parameter $\alpha(0 < \alpha < q)$ the elements of the decision vector $\bar{Y}_i$ corresponding to the received vector $\bar{\omega}_i$ are then given by

$$Y_i(j) = \begin{cases} 1 & \omega_i(j) \geq \tilde{\omega}_i(\alpha) \\ 0 & \omega_i(j) < \tilde{\omega}_i(\alpha) \end{cases} \tag{3}$$

Thus the receiver simply assigns 1's to the entries corresponding to the elements of the vector $\bar{\omega}_i$ that are greater than the αth element of the ordered series $\tilde{\omega}_i$ obtained by sorting the vector $\bar{\omega}_i$ in the descending order and zeros to the remaining elements of $\bar{Y}_i$. Therefore each vector $\bar{Y}_i$ has Hamming weight α. Since the positions of the nonzero entries in the vector $\bar{Y}_s$ (i.e. the numbers of subchannels chosen by the receiver) depend only on the distribution of the received vector elements and the user under consideration employs random permutations equiprobably chosen from the set of all possible permutations all the possible output vectors are equiprobable. Therefore the single user reception in the scenario under consideration can be described by $L(\alpha, p)$ channel. The value of the probability p depends both on the number of interfering signals and on the restrictions on the interfering signals' transmission. Please note that the subchannels via which the interfering signals are transmitted need not be chosen randomly since the receiver employs inverse permutations. The only important condition is that the permutations that are employed by the user should not be known to the interfering users.

We are aiming at finding the channel capacity of the $L(\alpha, p)$ channel.

3   Capacity of the Channel Under Consideration

Let us consider the channel model introduced above in more detail. First of all let as note that since each output vector $\bar{Y}_i$ depends only on the respective input vector $\bar{X}_i$ the $L(\alpha, p)$ channel is in fact a discrete memoryless channel (DMC). Let us consider a certain input vector $\bar{X}_i$ with a nonzero entry at the kth position (i.e. $X_i(k) = 1$). With probability p the transmission of this vector will result in reception of the vector $\bar{Y}_i$ for which (1) holds i.e. with probablity p the following holds $Y_i(k) = 1$. Let as designate the set of all vectors of Hamming weight α for which (1) holds with S_α^1 and the set of all the other vectors of Hamming weight α (i.e. those for which (2) holds) with S_α^0. Thus the transition probabilities for the DMC under consideration are given by:

$$p\left(\bar{Y}_i \in S_\alpha^1 \,\middle|\, \bar{X}_i\right) = \frac{p}{|S_\alpha^1|} = \frac{p}{C_{q-1}^{\alpha-1}} \tag{4}$$

and

$$p\left(\bar{Y}_i \in S_\alpha^0 \,\middle|\, \bar{X}_i\right) = \frac{1-p}{|S_\alpha^1|} = \frac{1-p}{C_{q-1}^{\alpha}} \tag{5}$$

respectively. Please note that (4) and (5) hold for any X_i and therefore the DMC under consideration is a symmetric one (vectors of transition probabilities for different inputs are permutations of each other) and the conditional entropy $H(Y|X)$ is therefore given by:

$$
\begin{aligned}
H(Y|X) &= \sum_{\bar{X}_i \in X} p\left(X = \bar{X}_i\right) H\left(Y \,\middle|\, X = \bar{X}_i\right) \\
&= H\left(Y \,\middle|\, X = \bar{X}_i\right) = \sum_{\bar{Y}_i \in Y} H\left(Y = \bar{Y}_i \,\middle|\, X = \bar{X}_i\right) = \\
&= \sum_{\bar{Y}_i \in S_\alpha^1} \left(Y = \bar{Y}_i \,\middle|\, X = \bar{X}_i\right) + \sum_{\bar{Y}_i \in S_\alpha^0} \left(Y = \bar{Y}_i \,\middle|\, X = \bar{X}_i\right) = \\
&= -p \log\left(\frac{p}{C_{q-1}^{\alpha-1}}\right) - (1-p) \log\left(\frac{1-p}{C_{q-1}^{\alpha}}\right) = \\
&= H(p) + \log\left(\frac{(q-1)!}{(q-\alpha-1)!(\alpha-1)!}\right) - \\
&\quad -p \log(q-\alpha) - (1-p) \log \alpha
\end{aligned}
\tag{6}
$$

It is well known [11] that the uniform input distribution is capacity achieving for symmetic DMCs. For the channel under consideration and a uniform input distribution the entropy of the output is given by:

$$
\begin{aligned}
H(Y)\Big|_{p(x_i)=\frac{1}{|X|}, \,\forall\, i=1:|X|} &= \log(|Y|) = \log\left(C_q^\alpha\right) = \\
&= \log\left(\frac{(q-1)!}{(q-\alpha-1)!(\alpha-1)!}\right) + \log(q) - \\
&\quad - \log(\alpha) - \log(q-\alpha)
\end{aligned}
\tag{7}
$$

and the capacity is given by

$$
\begin{aligned}
C = I(Y|X)\Big|_{p(x_i)=\frac{1}{|X|}, \,\forall\, i=1:|X|} &= \\
= \log(q) - p \log(\alpha) - (1-p) \log(q-\alpha) - H(p)
\end{aligned}
\tag{8}
$$

In the next section the obtained expression will be used to analyze the performance of the system employing the reception technique considered above.

4   Simulation

Let us consider the following scenario: assume that $\tilde{K} = K + 1$ active users transmit in a system with Q orthogonal subcarriers employing the transmission technique considered above. In what follows single user reception described above will be considered. Therefore signals transmitted by the other active users will be further on referred to as "interfering". Hereinafter it will be assumed that interfering signals power at the receiver end is $\varrho = 10^4$ times higher than that of the signal transmitted by the user under consideration. Moreover it will be assumed that apart from narrowband interfering signals the received signal is influenced by the background noise characterized by the signal-to-noise ratio given by $SNR = 10 * log_{10}(\frac{E_s}{E_N})$ where E_s is the energy of the signal transmitted by the user under consideration (at the receiver side) and E_N is noise energy (please note that E_N is noise energy in the entire band whereas E_s is the energy in the effective band occupied by the transmitted signal). We use simulation to compute the value of probability p for each value of α. The obtained values of p are then used to compute the capacity of the system employing reception technique under consideration by using (8). In Fig.1 dependencies of the channel capacity on the value of parameter α for different values of K and SNR are depicted the dependencies in Fig.1 demonstrate that the capacity of the system increases as K decreases and SNR increases. Moreover for any value of K and SNR there is a value of the parameter α that provides maximum value of channel capacity (for the sake of brevity we will further on call this value "optimal" and designate it with α_{opt}). It can be seen that as SNR decreases and K increases α_{opt} increases. On the other hand for a relatively wide range of nonoptimal values

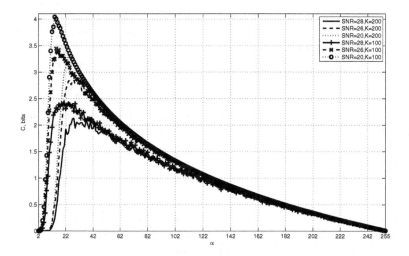

Fig. 1. Dependencies of the channel capacity on the value of parameter α for different values of K and SNR

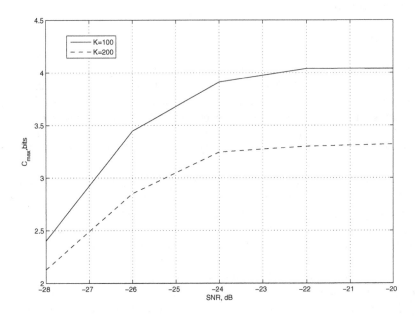

Fig. 2. Dependencies of C_{max} on the value of SNR for different values of K

of α the values of capacity for different values of K and SNR almost coincide i.e. even nonoptimal choice of α can ensure reliable communication at relatively low but nonzero transmission rates.

Let us now consider the value of the channel capacity that can be ensured by choosing $\alpha = \alpha_{opt}$. We shall designate it with C_{max}. In Fig.2 dependencies of C_{max} on the value of SNR for different values of K are presented.

As can be seen from Fig 2. the reception technique under consideration can provide reliable communication even under drastic interference. On the other hand it can be noted that the value $\eta = \frac{C_{max}}{log_2(q)}$ is relatively low (e.g. in the case considered in this section this value varies from 0.2661 to 0.5049) i.e. even for the system employing the robust reception technique under consideration severe interference leads to substantial performance degradation.

5   Conclusion

Hereinabove a single user receiver operating under multiuser interference and employing low complexity order statistics based receiver has been considered. In order to find the capacity of the resulting channel a vector channel model has been proposed. The model under consideration can be applied to describe a wide range of channel models. Explicit analytical expression for the capacity of the channel described by the proposed model has been obtained. To demonstrate the potential of the reception technique under consideration the obtained analytical expression has been used to analyze the performance of the system employing this technique.

References

1. Chang, S.C., Wolf, J.K.: On the T-User M-Frequency Noiseless Multiple-Access Channels with and without Intensity Information. IEEE Trans. Inform. Theory **27**(1), 41–48 (1981)
2. Wilhelmsson, L., Zigangirov, K.S.: On the Asymptotic Capacity of a Multiple-Access Channel. Probl. of Inf. Transm. **33**(1), 12–20 (1997)
3. Bassalygo, L.A., Pinsker, M.S.: Evaluation of the Asymptotics of the Summarized Capacity of an M-Frequency T-User Noiseless
4. Kreshchuk, A., Potapov, V.: New Coded Modulation for the Frequency Hoping OFDMA System. In: Thirteenth InternationalWorkshop on Algebraic and Combinational Coding Theory, Pomorje, Bulgaria, pp. 209–212, June 15–21, 2012
5. Kondrashov, K., Afanassiev, V.: Ordered statistics decoding for semi-orthogonal linear block codes over random non-Gaussian channels. In: Proc. of the Thirteenth International Workshop on Algebraic and Combinatorial Coding Theory, Pomorie, Bulgaria, pp. 192–196, June 15–21, 2012
6. Osipov, D.: Reduced-complexity robust detector in a DHA FH OFDMA system under mixed interference. In: Jonsson, M., Vinel, A., Bellalta, B., Belyaev, E. (eds.) MACOM 2014. LNCS, vol. 8715, pp. 29–34. Springer, Heidelberg (2014)
7. Zigangirov, K., Popov, A.S., Chepyzhov, V.: Nonbinary convolutional coding in channels with jamming. Problems of Information Transmission **31**(2), 169–183 (1995)
8. Win, M.Z., Scholtz, R.A.: Impulse Radio: How It Works. IEEE Communication Letter **2**(2), 36–38 (1998)
9. Arslan, H., Chen, Z.N., Di Benedetto, M.-G.: Ultra Wideband Wireless Communication. John Wiley & Sons (2006)
10. Weinstein, S., Ebert, P.: Data transmission by frequency-division multiplexing using the discrete Fourier transform. IEEE Trans. Commun. **19**, 628–634 (1971)
11. Gallager, R.G.: Information Theory and Reliable Communication. John Wiley & Sons Inc, New York (1968)

Fair Allocation of Throughput Under Harsh Operational Conditions

Andrey Garnaev[1,2]([✉]), Shweta Sagari[2], and Wade Trappe[2]

[1] Saint Petersburg State University, St Petersburg, Russia
garnaev@yahoo.com
[2] WINLAB, Rutgers University, North Brunswick, NJ, USA
shsagari@winlab.rutgers.edu,trappe@winlab.rutgers.edu

Abstract. Fairness plays an important role in networking as it fundamentally describes how different communication participants access and share network resources. The fair sharing of resources becomes complicated when the network faces harsh operational conditions, which may be associated with mutual interference or adversarial conditions. In this paper, we study the problem of fair allocation of resources in a network facing harsh operational conditions associated with communication transmission. Such a problem is becoming increasingly relevant in wireless system design as multiple wireless technologies are being deployed in shared spectrum, e.g. WiFi and LTE-U, and wireless networks are facing unprecedented levels of malicious activities. To obtain insight into this problem we suggest a simple game theoretical model involving resource allocation. We solve the game explicitly, which allows us to explore the structure of resource allocation strategies, and thereby provide guidance into the integration of fair resource allocation in networks.

Keywords: Fairness · Resource allocation · Jamming · Equilibrium

1 Introductions

Fairness is an important issue in wireless networks due to significant mismatch between resource requests and the available network capacity. Fairness concepts have been explored from several different directions in wireless systems, e.g., spectrum sharing, energy or network capacity sharing to achieve a required quality of service, etc. The use of fairness in network design pre-dates wireless systems, for example in the ATM standards [1], maxmin fairness and its weighted versions are used. Proportional fairness was introduced in [2], and later implemented in wireless systems (e.g. in the Qualcomm High Data Rate (HDR) scheduler) as a way to allocate throughput. As another example, a self-organizing network algorithm for virtual sectorization was constructed to maximize the proportional fair utility of all of the users' throughputs [3]. In [4], a general problem for fair throughput assignment (α-*fairness*) was suggested and, in particular, for particular values of α, α-fairness covers a wide array of fairness criteria,

© Springer International Publishing Switzerland 2015
M. Jonsson et al. (Eds.): MACOM 2015, LNCS 9305, pp. 108–119, 2015.
DOI: 10.1007/978-3-319-23440-3_9

including throughput maximization, proportionally fair assignment, delay minimization, and approximates maxmin fairness arbitrarily closely. In [5], it was used to improve resource allocation decisions in a particular type of Transmission Control Protocol (TCP) flows with any-increase/restarting dynamics. In [6], a generalized α-fairness concept was suggested and applied for the optimization of resource allocation in downlink cellular networks. In [7], a zero-sum game-theoretical model of power allocation was studied to maintain fair allocation of users's SNR (signal-to-noise ratio). Clearly, fairness has played a central role in communication system design, and a survey of further concepts related to fairness in wireless communication is given in [8].

Another important design consideration facing wireless networks is that they are built upon a shared and open medium. As a consequence, a major design consideration facing wireless networks is sharing access to the medium and coping with interference inherent in the wireless medium. Notably, wireless networks are susceptible to either malicious (say, jamming attack, as an example, see [9]) or natural (say, mutual interference between legitimate users of the same network or of different network, like LTE-U (LTE in unlicensed band) and WiFi, which share the same spectrum band) forms of interference. It is worth noting that beyond jamming, there are many other forms of malicious activities or security attacks in wireless networks that can affect the ability of users to utilize the medium. The reader can find comprehensive surveys of such threats in [10–13].

In this paper, we consider the problem of fair resource allocation under harsh operational conditions associated with communication transmission. In particular, we explore two issues jointly: fairness and network reliability. To obtain insight into this problem we suggest a simple maxmin problem which is equivalent to a zero sum game between a network's authority (e.g., a base station) and its rival (for a non-malicious case this may be viewed as *nature* causing harsh conditions, while for a malicious case this can be considered as an adversary). Thus, an important particular feature in our model is that the agents in the network have conflicting interests. Game theory [14] suggests a wide spectrum of approaches to formulate and solve such problems. In [15], one can find a structured and comprehensive survey of research contributions that analyze and solve security problems in wireless and computer networks via game-theoretic approaches. Here, as examples of game-theoretic approaches, we mention just a few such works: for modeling malicious users in collaborative networks [16], information warfare [17], for attack-type uncertainty on a network [18], for transmission under jamming [19], for ad hoc networks [20], for ALOHA networks [21], for bandwidth scanning [22,23], for network security [24,25], for a spectrum coexistence problem [26], for a smart jammer with end-user decision making is modeled using prospect theory [27], and for secret communication under uncertainty on the eavesdropper's capacity [28].

1.1 Organization of the Paper

The organization of this paper is as follows: in Section 2, we formulate the problem fair resource allocation as a zero-sum game. In Section 3, explicit equilibrium strategies for the problem are found when the adversary is not present in the network. In Section 4, the problem is solved when the adversary is present in the network. Finally, in Section 5, an important particular subcase is considered and conclusions are given.

2   The Problem

In this paper, we consider the fair allocation of resources by a base station BS while facing *operational* noise affecting transmission reliability. A strategy of the BS is a power allocation vector $\boldsymbol{P} = (P_1, \ldots, P_n)$, describing how power is allocated across *channels* or *time slots* or *users*, such that $P_i \geq 0$ for $i \in$ in$\{1, 2, \ldots, n\}$ and $\sum_{i=1}^{n} P_i = \overline{P}$, where $\overline{P}$ is the total power the BS has to distribute across the set of channels. As noted, such a strategy can be interpreted in the following two ways (Figure 1):

(i) The total power $\overline{P}$ has to be transmitted across n channels or time slots,
(ii) The total power $\overline{P}$ has to be assigned to n users.

Much of the discussion that follows will refer to the *user* case.

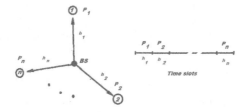

Fig. 1. Two interpretation of the strategy

As a payoff to the BS we consider the α-fairness utility function of the users's or channel/time slot throughput $u_i(P_i) = \ln\left(1 + \frac{h_i P_i}{\sigma^2}\right)$, i.e.,

$$v(\boldsymbol{P}) = \frac{1}{1-\alpha} \sum_{i=1}^{n} \ln^{1-\alpha}\left(1 + \frac{h_i P_i}{\sigma^2}\right) \quad \text{for } \alpha \neq 1 \tag{1}$$

and

$$v(\boldsymbol{P}) = \sum_{i=1}^{n} \ln\left(\ln\left(1 + \frac{h_i P_i}{\sigma^2}\right)\right) \quad \text{for } \alpha = 1, \tag{2}$$

where σ^2 is the background noise, $h_i > 0$ are fading channel gains, and $\alpha \geq 0$ is the fairness coefficient.

This parameter allows one to treat in the same universal formulation several important particular cases. The case $\alpha = 0$ corresponds to maximization of total throughput. The case $\alpha = 2$ corresponds to minimization of total delay (sum of inverse values of throughput) in transmission. The case $\alpha = 1$ corresponds to the Nash bargaining [14] problem for throughput with transferable total power. Let us discuss the last case in detail. The assumption about the transferable total power means that the BS can redistribute the total power, in which case the Nash bargaining solution is given by the power allocation $\boldsymbol{P}$ maximizing the Nash product

$$p(\boldsymbol{P}) := \prod_{i=1}^{n}(u_i(P_i) - u_i(0)) = \prod_{i=1}^{n}\ln\left(1 + \frac{h_i P_i}{\sigma^2}\right). \tag{3}$$

Since $\ln(x)$ is increasing in x, the Nash bargaining solution can be found as the power allocation $\boldsymbol{P}$ maximizing the sum of the logarithm of throughput, i.e., $\sum_{i=1}^{n}\ln\left(\ln\left(1 + \frac{h_i P_i}{\sigma^2}\right)\right)$. This coincides with α-fairness utility (2) for $\alpha = 1$.

Beyond the background noise, an induced noise of the total power $\overline{J}$, caused by nature or by an adversary, can be present in the network. In our model, the BS knows only its total value, but does not know its allocation across channels, slots or users.

For the sake of uniform presentation, a source of the induced nose will be referred to as an adversary. The goal of the BS is to maximize fairness allocation of the total power under harsh operational conditions. To deal with this situation we introduce a strategy for the adversary as $\boldsymbol{J} = (J_1, \ldots, J_n)$, where $J_i \geq 0$ is the power applied to jam user i (within time slot i), and $\sum_{i=1}^{n} J_i = \overline{J}$, where $\overline{J}$ is the total jamming power. Then, the payoff of the BS in the presence of such adversary's activity is

$$v(\boldsymbol{P}, \boldsymbol{J}) = \frac{1}{1-\alpha}\sum_{i=1}^{n}\ln^{1-\alpha}\left(1 + \frac{h_i P_i}{\sigma^2 + g_i J_i}\right) \quad \text{for } \alpha \neq 1 \tag{4}$$

and

$$v(\boldsymbol{P}, \boldsymbol{J}) = \sum_{i=1}^{n}\ln\left(\ln\left(1 + \frac{h_i P_i}{\sigma^2 + g_i J_i}\right)\right) \quad \text{for } \alpha = 1. \tag{5}$$

We assume that all of the fading channel gains g_i, h_i and the the background noise σ^2, the total power resources $\overline{P}$ of the BS as well as the total noise $\overline{J}$ induced by the adversary are fixed and known to the BS. We thus have to find the resource allocation protocol under the harsh conditions, i.e., $\boldsymbol{P} = \arg\max_{\boldsymbol{P}} \min_{\boldsymbol{J}} v(\boldsymbol{P}, \boldsymbol{J})$,

3   The Adversary is Not Present

In the case where the adversary is not present, i.e., the total jamming power is zero, the optimal power allocation is given by $\boldsymbol{P} = \arg\max_{\boldsymbol{P}} v(\boldsymbol{P})$.

Theorem 1. *If the jammer is not present then the optimal jammer strategy* $\boldsymbol{P} = \boldsymbol{P}(\omega)$ *is given as follows:*

$$P_i(\omega) := \begin{cases} \dfrac{\sigma^2}{h_i} F_\alpha^{-1}\left(\dfrac{h_i}{\sigma^2}\omega\right), & \alpha > 0, \\ \left\lfloor \dfrac{1}{\omega} - \dfrac{\sigma^2}{h_i} \right\rfloor_+, & \alpha = 0 \end{cases} \tag{6}$$

with $\lfloor x \rfloor_+ = \max\{x, 0\}$ *and*

$$F_\alpha(x) := \frac{1}{(1+x)\ln^\alpha(1+x)}, \tag{7}$$

where ω *is a unique positive root of the equation:*

$$\sum_{i=1}^n P_i(\omega) = \overline{P}. \tag{8}$$

In particular, if $\alpha > 0$ then $P_i(\omega) > 0$ for each user i. So, each user gets a power supply. If $\alpha = 0$ then the optimal *BS* strategy has a water-filling form [29]. Namely, the *BS* assigns the power supply only to the users with good quality of the channels, i.e., for the users with enough big induced fading channel gain h_i/σ^2. Figure 2 illustrates this phenomena for $n = 3$ and $h = (3, 1, 2)$ and $\sigma^2 = 1$. For $\overline{P} \leq 1.05$ and $\alpha = 0$, $P_2 = 0$. Increasing total power $\overline{P}$ yields increasing all the components of the optimal strategy $\boldsymbol{P}$ for all α.

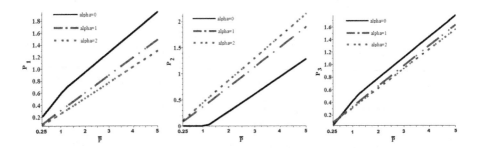

Fig. 2. The optimal strategy $\boldsymbol{P}$ for $\overline{P} \in [0.25, 5]$ and $\alpha = 0, 1, 2$

4   The Adversary is Present

In this section we consider the situation where the adversary is present, i.e., the interference power $\overline{J} > 0$. We can describe the maxmin problem as a zero sum game where the *BS* wants to maximize its payoff, meanwhile the adversary wants to minimize it. We are looking for equilibrium strategies. Recall that $(\boldsymbol{P}_*, \boldsymbol{J}_*)$ are the equilibrium strategies (for zero-sum game such strategies also are called *saddle point*) if and only if the following inequalities are hold for any $(\boldsymbol{P}, \boldsymbol{J})$

$$v(\boldsymbol{P}, \boldsymbol{J}_*) \leq v(\boldsymbol{P}_*, \boldsymbol{J}_*) \leq v(\boldsymbol{P}_*, \boldsymbol{J}). \tag{9}$$

Theorem 2. *The game has at least one equilibrium for $\alpha \leq 2$.*

To obtain the equilibrium strategies, first we describe, in Lemma 1, the structure of the equilibrium strategies as functions of two auxiliary parameters (being Lagrange multipliers of the corresponding optimization problems). Then, in Lemma 2, monotonic properties of these strategies will be established. This will allow, in Theorem 3, to reduce the problem of finding the equilibrium strategies to solving an equation of one variable.

Lemma 1. *Each equilibrium has the form $(\boldsymbol{P}(\omega,\nu), \boldsymbol{J}(\omega,\nu))$ with*

$$
P_i(\omega,\nu) =
\begin{cases}
\dfrac{h_i}{g_i} \dfrac{\dfrac{\nu}{\omega^2}}{\ln^\alpha \left(1 + \dfrac{h_i}{g_i}\dfrac{\nu}{\omega}\right)\left(1 + \dfrac{h_i}{g_i}\dfrac{\nu}{\omega}\right)}, & i \notin I_0(\omega,\nu), \\[4ex]
\dfrac{h_i}{\sigma^2} F_\alpha^{-1}\left(\dfrac{\sigma^2}{h_i}\omega\right), & i \in I_0(\omega,\nu),
\end{cases}
\tag{10}
$$

$$
J_i(\omega,\nu) =
\begin{cases}
\dfrac{h_i}{g_i} \dfrac{\dfrac{1}{\omega}}{\ln^\alpha \left(1 + \dfrac{h_i}{g_i}\dfrac{\nu}{\omega}\right)\left(1 + \dfrac{h_i}{g_i}\dfrac{\nu}{\omega}\right)} - \dfrac{\sigma^2}{g_i}, & i \notin I_0(\omega,\nu), \\[4ex]
0, & i \in I_0(\omega,\nu)
\end{cases}
\tag{11}
$$

with

$$
I_0(\omega,\nu) := \left\{ i : \dfrac{g_i}{h_i}\omega F_\alpha^{-1}\left(\dfrac{h_i}{\sigma^2}\omega\right) \leq \nu \right\}.
\tag{12}
$$

Lemma 2. *Let*

$$
S_P(\omega,\nu) := \sum_{i=1}^{n} P_i(\omega,\nu) \ \text{ and } \ S_J(\omega,\nu) := \sum_{i=1}^{n} J_i(\omega,\nu).
\tag{13}
$$

Then, $S_P(\omega,\nu)$ and $S_J(\omega,\nu)$ are continuous in $\omega > 0$ and $\nu > 0$. Also,
  (J_1) For each $\omega > 0$, $S_J(\omega,\nu)$ is decreasing in ν.
  (J_2) For each fixed $\nu > 0$ and $\alpha \geq 1$, $S_J(\omega,\nu)$ is increasing in ω.
  (J_3) For each fixed $\nu > 0$ and $\alpha = 0$, $S_J(\omega,\nu)$ is decreasing in ω.
  (P_1) For each $\nu > 0$, $S_P(\omega,\nu)$ is decreasing in ω.
  (P_2) For each fixed $\omega > 0$ and $\alpha \geq 1$, $S_P(\omega,\nu)$ is decreasing in ν.
  (P_3) For each fixed $\omega > 0$ and $\alpha = 0$, $S_P(\omega,\nu)$ is increasing in ν.

Based on Lemma 13 and Lemma 2 the following theorem follows.

Theorem 3. *Each equilibrium has the form given by Lemma 1, where $\omega = \omega(\nu)$ for each ν is a unique solution of the equation*

$$
S_P(\omega,\nu) = \overline{P}.
$$

Meanwhile, ν is a root of the equation

$$S_J(\omega(\nu), \nu) = \overline{J}.$$

The function $\omega(\nu)$ is increasing in ν for $\alpha = 0$, and decreasing in ν for $\alpha \in [1, 2]$. For both these cases $S_J(\omega(\nu), \nu)$ is decreasing in ν, and, thus, ν is uniquely defined. For $\alpha \in (0, 1)$, uniqueness of ν is not guaranteed. If multiple roots for ν arise, they return equivalent strategies from the BS point of view since each of them return the same payoff to the BS. Of course, for $\alpha = 0$ and $\alpha \in [1, 2]$, the bisection method to find the optimal ν can be used due to the monotonic property of $S_J(\omega(\nu), \nu)$.

5   A Particular Case and Conclusions

In particular cases associated with a high SINR regime, the throughput may be approximated by $\ln(1 + h_i P_i/(\sigma^2 + g_i J_i)) \approx \ln(h_i P_i/(\sigma^2 + g_i J_i))$ for any i, and then the equilibrium strategies can be simplified.

If $\alpha = 0$ then the *BS* equilibrium strategy is a uniform power allocation

$$P_i = \overline{P}/n \text{ for } i \in \{1, 2, \dots, n\},$$

and the adversary strategy has a water-filling form depending only on the adversary's fading channel gains, and it is given by

$$J_i = \lfloor 1/\nu - \sigma^2/g_i \rfloor_+ \text{ for } i \in \{1, 2, \dots, n\},$$

where ν is such that $\sum_{i=1}^{n} \lfloor 1/\nu - \sigma^2/g_i \rfloor_+ = \overline{J}$.

If $\alpha > 0$, then the equilibrium strategies $\boldsymbol{P}$ and $\boldsymbol{J}$ have the form

$$P_i = \begin{cases} \dfrac{\sigma^2}{h_i}\left(F_\alpha^{-1}\left(\dfrac{h_i}{\sigma^2}\omega\right) - 1\right), & \dfrac{1}{\nu \ln^\alpha((h_i/g_i)(\nu/\omega))} \le \dfrac{\sigma^2}{g_i}, \\ \dfrac{1}{\omega \ln^\alpha((h_i/g_i)(\nu/\omega))}, & \dfrac{1}{\nu \ln^\alpha((h_i/g_i)(\nu/\omega))} > \dfrac{\sigma^2}{g_i}, \end{cases}$$

$$J_i = \left\lfloor \dfrac{1}{\nu \ln^\alpha((h_i/g_i)(\nu/\omega))} - \dfrac{\sigma^2}{g_i} \right\rfloor_+ \text{ for } i \in \{1, 2, \dots, n\}.$$

Note that the other important particular case of this problem, namely, low SINR regime was studied for optimization α-fairness in [7] and for optimization total SINR in [30].

If the fading channel gains are proportional, i.e., $f_i/g_i = r$ for any i, we can observe a quite surprising stability associated with the optimal jamming power allocation strategy for high and regular SINR regimes. Namely, it does not depend on the fairness coefficient. Figure 3 illustrates the dependence of equilibrium strategies on increasing total jamming power $\overline{J}$.

Finally, we note the obtained results have allowed us to illustrate the essential difference between the throughput maximization and fair allocation throughput problems in harsh operational conditions, i.e., when noise allocation between

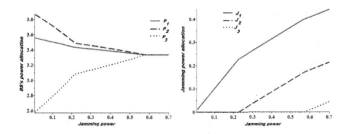

Fig. 3. Two interpretation of strategies

users or time slots is unknown. One such difference could have been expected at the outset. Namely, for the fair allocation throughput problem all the users will obtain power allocated to them, while in the throughput maximization problem only the users with good network characteristics will be supplied with power. Of course, power allocation between users essentially depends on the total jamming power. The other difference is not as intuitive and may be considered unexpected. In the high SINR regime, in the throughput's maximization problem, the BS does not take into account the difference in the user's network characteristics. It applies uniform power allocation strategies. Meanwhile, in the fair allocation throughput problem, the BS assigns power to the users according to their characteristics. It also shows difference between high and regular SINR regimes since in high SINR regime in both optimization problems all of the users obtain power, while in SINR regimes this occurs only for the fair allocation throughput problem.

6 Appendix

6.1 Proof of Theorem 2

Note that

$$\frac{\partial^2 v(\boldsymbol{P}, \boldsymbol{J})}{\partial P_i^2} = -\frac{h_i^2}{(\sigma^2 + h_i P_i + g_i J_i)^2} \frac{\alpha + \ln\left(1 + \frac{h_i P_i}{\sigma^2 + g_i J_i}\right)}{\ln^{1+\alpha}\left(1 + \frac{h_i P_i}{\sigma^2 + g_i J_i}\right)} < 0 \qquad (14)$$

and

$$\frac{\partial^2 v(\boldsymbol{P}, \boldsymbol{J})}{\partial J_i^2} = \frac{h_i g_i P_i}{(\sigma^2 + g_i J_i)(\sigma^2 + h_i P_i + g_i J_i)^2} \frac{G\left(\frac{h_i P_i}{\sigma^2 + g_i J_i}\right)}{\ln^{1+\alpha}\left(1 + \frac{h_i P_i}{\sigma^2 + g_i J_i}\right)}, \qquad (15)$$

where $G(x) = (2 + x)\ln(1 + x) - \alpha x$.
It is clear that $G(x)$ is positive if $\alpha \leq 2$ due to $G(0) = 0$ and

$$\frac{dG}{dx} = \ln(1 + x) + \frac{1}{1 + x} + 1 - \alpha \geq \min_{x \geq 0}\left(\ln(1 + x) + \frac{1}{1 + x}\right) + 1 - \alpha = 2 - \alpha. \qquad (16)$$

Thus, $v(\boldsymbol{P}, \boldsymbol{J})$ is concave in $\boldsymbol{P}$ and convex in $\boldsymbol{J}$ for $\alpha \leq 2$. By [14], the result follows. ∎

6.2   Proof of Theorem 1

To find the optimal resource allocation the Lagrangian has to be defined:
$L_\omega(P) = v(P, 0) + \omega \left(\overline{P} - \sum_{i=1}^{n} P_i \right)$. Note that $\frac{\partial L_\omega(P)}{\partial P_i} = \frac{h_i}{\sigma^2} F_\alpha \left(\frac{h_i P_i}{\sigma^2} \right) - \omega$ with
$F_\alpha(x)$ given by (7).

For $\alpha > 0$, $F(x)$ is positive in $(0, \infty)$, and it is decreasing, and $F(x) \uparrow \infty$ for
$x \downarrow 0$ and $F(x) \downarrow 0$ for $x \uparrow \infty$. Thus, there is a unique optimal power allocation
P given by (6) and (8). For $\alpha = 0$, $F(x)$ is positive in $(0, \max_i(h_i/\sigma^2))$, and it
is decreasing from infinity for $x \downarrow 0$ to zero for $x = \max_i(h_i/\sigma^2)$, and the result
follows.   ∎

6.3   Proof of Lemma 1

By the definition of equilibrium (9), (P_*, J_*) is an equilibrium if and only if
they are a solution of the best response equations: $P_* = \max_P v(P, J_*)$ and
$J_* = \min_J v(P_*, J)$.

To deal with these two non-linear programming problems the Lagrangian
must be defined for each of them: $L_\omega^P(P) = v(P, J) + \omega \left(\overline{P} - \sum_{i=1}^{n} P_i \right)$ and
$L_\nu^J(J) = -v(P, J) + \nu \left(\overline{J} - \sum_{i=1}^{n} J_i \right)$.

Taking derivatives of the Lagrangian $\frac{\partial L_\omega^P}{\partial P_i}$ and $\frac{\partial L_\nu^J}{\partial J_i}$ imply that (P, J) is an
equilibrium if and only if the following relations hold:

$$\frac{1}{\ln^\alpha \left(1 + \frac{h_i P_i}{\sigma^2 + g_i J_i} \right)} \frac{h_i}{\sigma^2 + h_i P_i + g_i J_i} \begin{cases} = \omega, & P_i > 0, \\ \leq \omega, & P_i = 0 \end{cases} \tag{17}$$

and

$$\frac{1}{\ln^\alpha \left(1 + \frac{h_i P_i}{\sigma^2 + g_i J_i} \right)} \frac{h_i g_i P_i}{(\sigma^2 + h_i P_i + g_i J_i)(\sigma^2 + g_i J_i)} \begin{cases} = \nu, & J_i > 0, \\ \leq \nu, & J_i = 0. \end{cases} \tag{18}$$

(a) Let $\alpha > 0$. Then, by (17), $P_i > 0$ for all i. So, only two subcases might
arise (a_i) $J_i = 0$ and (a_{ii}) $J_i > 0$.

(a_i) Let $J_i = 0$. Then, by (17) and (18),

$$\frac{1}{\ln^\alpha \left(1 + \frac{h_i P_i}{\sigma^2} \right)} \frac{h_i}{\sigma^2 + h_i P_i} = \omega, \tag{19}$$

and

$$\frac{1}{\ln^\alpha \left(1 + \frac{h_i P_i}{\sigma^2} \right)} \frac{h_i g_i P_i}{(\sigma^2 + h_i P_i)\sigma^2} \leq \nu. \tag{20}$$

Thus,

$$P_i = P_i(\omega) := \frac{\sigma^2}{h_i} F_\alpha^{-1}\left(\frac{h_i}{\sigma^2}\omega\right) \tag{21}$$

and

$$\frac{g_i}{h_i}\omega F_\alpha^{-1}\left(\frac{h_i}{\sigma^2}\omega\right) \leq \nu. \tag{22}$$

(a_{ii}) Let $J_i > 0$. Then, by (17) and (18),

$$\frac{1}{\ln^\alpha\left(1 + \dfrac{h_i P_i}{\sigma^2 + g_i J_i}\right)} \frac{h_i}{\sigma^2 + h_i P_i + g_i J_i} = \omega, \tag{23}$$

and

$$\frac{1}{\ln^\alpha\left(1 + \dfrac{h_i P_i}{\sigma^2 + g_i J_i}\right)} \frac{h_i g_i P_i}{(\sigma^2 + h_i P_i + g_i J_i)(\sigma^2 + g_i J_i)} = \nu. \tag{24}$$

Dividing (24) by (23) and multiplying both sides of the obtained equality by $(\sigma^2 + g_i J_i)$ imply

$$g_i P_i = \frac{\nu}{\omega}(\sigma^2 + g_i J_i). \tag{25}$$

Substituting $\sigma^2 + g_i J_i$ into (23) yields

$$P_i = \frac{h_i}{g_i} \frac{\dfrac{\nu}{\omega^2}}{\ln^\alpha\left(1 + \dfrac{h_i}{g_i}\dfrac{\nu}{\omega}\right)\left(1 + \dfrac{h_i}{g_i}\dfrac{\nu}{\omega}\right)}. \tag{26}$$

Then, (25) and (26) imply

$$J_i = \frac{h_i}{g_i} \frac{\dfrac{1}{\omega}}{\ln^\alpha\left(1 + \dfrac{h_i}{g_i}\dfrac{\nu}{\omega}\right)\left(1 + \dfrac{h_i}{g_i}\dfrac{\nu}{\omega}\right)} - \frac{\sigma^2}{g_i}. \tag{27}$$

and the result follows.   ∎

7   Proof of Lemma 2

Let $M_k = \frac{x^k}{\ln^\alpha(1+x)(1+x)}$ with $k = 1, 2$. First prove that

(a) If $\alpha \in [0, 2]$ then M_2 is increasing in x,
(b) If $\alpha \in [1, 2]$ then M_1 is decreasing in x,
(c) If $\alpha \in (0, 1)$ then M_1 is increasing in x for $x < x_\alpha$ and decreasing for $x > x_\alpha$, where x_α is a unique positive root of the equation $\ln(1 + x) = \alpha x$ for $\alpha \in (0, 1)$, i.e., $x_\alpha = -(\alpha + \text{LambertW}(-1, -\alpha/\exp(\alpha)))/\alpha$,
(d) If $\alpha = 0$ then M_1 is increasing in x.

Note that $\frac{dM_2}{dx} = \frac{x((2+x)\ln(1+x)-\alpha x)}{\ln^\alpha(1+x)(1+x)^2} > 0$ for $\alpha \in [0,2]$. Also, $\frac{dM_1}{dx} = \frac{\ln(1+x)-\alpha x}{\ln^\alpha(1+x)(1+x)^2}$. This implies that

$$\frac{dM_1}{dx} \begin{cases} < 0, & \alpha \geq 1, \\ > 0, & \alpha \in (0,1), x < x_\alpha, \\ < 0, & \alpha \in (0,1), x > x_\alpha, \\ > 0, & \alpha = 0. \end{cases}$$

Hence, (a)-(d) follow. Then, (a)-(d) jointly with (1) imply the result. ∎

References

1. The ATM forum Technical Committee: Traffic management specification (April 1996). http://www.broadband-forum.org/ftp/pub/approved-specs/af-tm-0056.000.pdf (version 4.0)
2. Kelly, F.P.: Charging and rate control for elastic traffic. European Trans. on Telecom. **8**, 33–37 (1998)
3. Tall, A., Altman, Z., Altman, E.: Virtual sectorization: design and self-optimization. In: 5th International Workshop on Self-Organizing Networks (IWSON) (2015)
4. Mo, J., Walrand, J.: Fair end-to-end window-based congestion control. IEEE/ACM Trans. on Networking **8**, 556–567 (2000)
5. Jacko, P., Sanso, B.: Optimal anticipative congestion control of flows with time-varying input stream. Performance Evaluation **69**, 86–101 (2012)
6. Altman, E., Avrachenkov, K., Garnaev, A.: Generalized α-fair resource allocation in wireless networks. In: Proceedings of 47th IEEE Conference on Decision and Control (CDC 2008), pp. 2414–2419 (2008)
7. Altman, E., Avrachenkov, K., Garnaev, A.: Fair resource allocation in wireless networks in the presence of a jammer. Performance Evaluation **67**, 338–349 (2010)
8. Huaizhou, S., Prasad, R.V., Onur, E., Niemegeers, I.G.M.M.: Fairness in wireless networks:issues, measures and challenges. IEEE Communications Surveys & Tutorials **16**, 5–24 (2014)
9. Lyamin, N., Vinel, A., Jonsson, M., Loo, J.: Real-time detection of denial-of-service attacks in IEEE 802.11p vehicular networks. IEEE Communications letters **18**, 110–113 (2014)
10. Park, J.-M., Reed, J.H., Clancy, T.C.: Security and enforcement in spectrum sharing. Proceedings of the IEEE **102** (2014)
11. Bhattacharjee, S., Sengupta, S., Chatterjee, M.: Vulnerabilities in cognitive radio networks: A survey. Computer Communications **36**, 1387–1398 (2013)
12. El-Hajj, W., Safa, H., Guizani, M.: Survey of security issues in cognitive radio networks. Journal of Internet Technology **12** (2012)
13. Khare, A., Saxena, M., Thakur, R.S., Chourasia, K.: Attacks and preventions of cognitive radio network-a survey. International Journal of Advanced Research in Computer Engineering and Technology **2** (2013)
14. Fudenberg, D., Tirole, J.: Game theory. MIT Press, Boston (1991)
15. Manshaei, M.H., Zhu, Q., Alpcan, T., Basar, T., Hubaux, J.-P.: Game theory meets network security and privacy. ACM Computing Survey **45** (2013)

16. Theodorakopoulos, G., Baras, J.S.: Game theoretic modeling of malicious users in collaborative networks. IEEE Journal on Selected Areas in Communications **26**, 1317–1327 (2008)
17. Hamilton, S.N., Miller, W.L., Ott, A., Saydjari, O.S.: Challenges to applying game theory to the domain of information warfare. In: Proceedings of ISW 2002 (2002)
18. Garnaev, A., Baykal-Gursoy, M., Poor, H.V.: Incorporating attack-type uncertainty into network protection. IEEE Transactions on Information Forensics and Security **9**, 1278–1287 (2014)
19. Garnaev, A., Hayel, Y., Altman, E., Avrachenkov, K.: Jamming game in a dynamic slotted ALOHA network. In: Jain, R., Kannan, R. (eds.) Gamenets 2011. LNICST, vol. 75, pp. 429–443. Springer, Heidelberg (2012)
20. Liu, Y., Comaniciu, C., Mani, H.: A Bayesian game approach for intrusion detection in wireless ad hoc networks. In: Proceedings of Valuetools 2006 (2006)
21. Sagduyu, Y.E., Ephremidess, A.: A game-theoretic analysis of denial of service attacks in wireless random access. Journal of Wireless Networks **15**, 651–666 (2009)
22. Garnaev, A., Trappe, W.: Stationary equilibrium strategies for bandwidth scanning. In: Jonsson, M., Vinel, A., Bellalta, B., Marina, N., Dimitrova, D., Fiems, D. (eds.) MACOM 2013. LNCS, vol. 8310, pp. 168–183. Springer, Heidelberg (2013)
23. Garnaev, A., Trappe, W., Kung, C.-T.: Dependence of optimal monitoring strategy on the application to be protected. In: Proceedings of 2012 IEEE Global Communications Conference (GLOBECOM), pp. 1054–1059 (2012)
24. Nguyen, K.C., Alpcan, T., Basar, T.: Stochastic games for security in networks with interdependent nodes. In: Proceedings of GAMENETS 2009, pp. 697–703 (2009)
25. Calinescu, G., Kapoor, S., Qiao, K., Shin, J.: Stochastic strategic routing reduces attack effects. In: Proceedings of GLOBECOM 2011, pp. 1–5 (2011)
26. Garnaev, A., Trappe, W.: One-time spectrum coexistence in dynamic spectrum access when the secondary user may be malicious. IEEE Transactions on Information Forensics and Security **10**, 1064–1075 (2015)
27. Xiao, L., Liu, J., Li, Y., Mandayam, N.B., Poor, H.V.: Prospect theoretic analysis of anti-jamming communications in cognitive radio networks. In: 2014 IEEE Global Communications Conference (GLOBECOM), pp. 746–751 (2014)
28. Garnaev, A., Trappe, W.: Secret communication when the eavesdropper might be an active adversary. In: Jonsson, M., Vinel, A., Bellalta, B., Belyaev, E. (eds.) MACOM 2014. LNCS, vol. 8715, pp. 121–136. Springer, Heidelberg (2014)
29. Garnaev, A., Hayel, Y., Altman, E.: Closed form solutions for symmetric water filling games. In: Proceedings of the 27th IEEE Communications Society Conference on Computer Communications (INFOCOM 2008), pp. 673–681 (2008)
30. Altman, E., Avrachenkov, K., Garnaev, A.: Transmission power control game with SINR as objective function. In: Altman, E., Chaintreau, A. (eds.) NET-COOP 2008. LNCS, vol. 5425, pp. 112–120. Springer, Heidelberg (2009)

MAC II

Near-Optimal Resource Allocation in Cooperative Cellular Networks Using Genetic Algorithms

Zihan Luo[(✉)], Simon Armour, and Joe McGeehan

Department of Electrical and Electronic Engineering, University of Bristol,
Bristol BS8 1UB, UK
{Zihan.Luo,Simon.Armour,J.P.McGeehan}@bristol.ac.uk

Abstract. This paper shows how a genetic algorithm can be used as a method of obtaining the near-optimal solution of the resource block scheduling problem in a cooperative cellular network. An exhaustive search is initially implemented to guarantee that the optimal result, in terms of maximizing the bandwidth efficiency of the overall network, is found, and then the genetic algorithm with the properly selected termination conditions is used in the same network. The simulation results show that the genetic algorithm can approximately achieve the optimum bandwidth efficiency whilst requiring only 24% of the computation effort of the exhaustive search in the investigated network.

Keywords: Multi-cell · Exhaustive search · Genetic algorithm · Frequency reuse · Cooperative transmission

1 Introduction

The optimal solution of resource scheduling is considered difficult to obtain given that it is a nonconvex problem [1,2,3,4]. Previous research work has investigated near-optimal algorithms for scheduling channels or subcarriers under the conditions of fairness and power control [5,6,7,8]. The general optimal solution without those conditions for scheduling resource blocks in a multi-cell network is not well-studied. The exhaustive search technique is commonly used for getting the optimal solution [5], [9]. However, it requires high computational effort to obtain the optimal results as it needs to search all the possible combinations or cases [1], [16]. The genetic algorithm is also a search method for solving nonconvex problems, and it is widely used in the fields such as cloud design, computing, sub-carrier allocation and even project management [11,12,13,14,15,16]. But it is rarely used in resource block scheduling to get as much bandwidth efficiency as possible for a downlink transmission in a multi-cell scenario. Ref. [15] proposed a genetic algorithm for resource block scheduling in the uplink transmission in a single cell model. The search of the genetic algorithm in [15] was stopped by the maximal number of iterations, so the resultant solution gives worse results than the optimum. This contribution investigates the use of genetic algorithm as a solution for getting the optimal bandwidth efficiency by scheduling resource blocks in a cooperative cellular network with the possibility of flexible

© Springer International Publishing Switzerland 2015
M. Jonsson et al. (Eds.): MACOM 2015, LNCS 9305, pp. 123–134, 2015.
DOI: 10.1007/978-3-319-23440-3_10

cooperation. The termination conditions used in the genetic algorithm are properly selected in order to get the optimal solution. The exhaustive search is used to get the optimal results in a 3-cell network layout, and the results from the genetic algorithm applied to the same network and the same user locations are compared with the optimal results. In addition, the computation effort of getting the optimal results by these two methods is compared.

This paper is organized as follows: section 2 and 3 display the system model and the problem statement; section 4 introduces how to get the optimal solution by the exhaustive search; section 5 explains the implementation of the genetic algorithm; section 6 compares and discusses the simulation results and section 7 presents the conclusion.

2   System Model

2.1   Network Layout

The system investigated is a downlink transmission in a hexagonal cellular network. There are in total M resource blocks to be scheduled to at most a total of U users in an N-cell layout. One Base Station (BS) is located in the center of each cell. A Resource Block (RB) is assumed to be the smallest resource unit to be scheduled and it can only be used once by each BS. The power of each RB is assumed to be the same. Frequency reuse is flexible which means that one RB can be used by more than one BS to schedule to the same user (cooperative transmission) or be used by different base stations to schedule to different users (frequency reuse).

The settings used in the simulation are for a typical LTE urban macro environment which are listed in Table 1 [10].

Table 1. Parameter Settings

Parameter	Value
Network layout	Hexagonal 3 cells
Cell radius	500m
Antenna	Omnidirectional
Carrier frequency	2GHz
Bandwidth	10MHz
Bandwidth per RB	180KHz
Number of available RBs	50
Distance-dependent path loss	$128.1+37.6*\log_{10}(d)$ with d in km
Thermal noise power spectral density	-174dBm/Hz
Maximum BS transmit power	40 watts
Mobile station noise figure	9dB
Minimum distance between user and BS	35 m

3   Problem Statement

This paper investigates the optimal solution of getting the total bandwidth efficiency by scheduling M resource blocks to at most U users in a layout of N cells. The SINR expression for the uth user in the mth RB with flexible frequency reuse is

$$S'_{u,m} = \frac{\sum\limits_{n \in \Omega_n} P_{u,n}}{N_s + \sum\limits_{n' \in \Omega_{n'}} P_{u,n'}}, \quad \Omega_n, \Omega_{n'} \subseteq [1, N] \tag{1}$$

where $P_{u,n} = P_m / P_{Lu,n}$ (P_m is the transmit power in the mth RB; $P_{Lu,n}$ is the path loss from the uth user to the nth BS) represents the received power of the uth user from the nth BS. Ω_n is the set of base stations that use the mth RB to transmit signals to the uth user (cooperative transmission occurs if there are more than one BS in this set) while $\Omega_{n'}$ stands for the set of the base stations that also use the mth RB but to transmit to the other users in the network. The base stations in Ω_n and $\Omega_{n'}$ are from 1 to N, and no elements may overlap between Ω_n and $\Omega_{n'}$. N_s is the noise power. (1) shows the SINR expression for the case that the mth RB is scheduled for the transmission between the base stations in the set of Ω_n to the uth user, whilst the mth RB is also used by the base stations in the set of $\Omega_{n'}$ but to transmit to the other users in the network as the interference to the uth user.

The capacity of the uth user in the mth resource block is

$$C_{u,m} = B_m \log_2(1 + S'_{u,m}), \tag{2}$$

where B_m is the bandwidth of the mth RB (180KHz in LTE). Thus, the total bandwidth efficiency of the N-cell layout with U users in total and M resource blocks in total (M≤50) is

$$P_{total} = \frac{1}{B_{total}} \sum_{u=1}^{U} \sum_{m=1}^{M} C_{u,m}, \tag{3}$$

where B_{total} is the total bandwidth used in the scheduling problem ($B_{total} \leq 10$MHz). The objective formula of this resource block scheduling problem (which to obtain the maximum total bandwidth efficiency for the network) is

$$\arg\max_{u,m,n} \frac{1}{B_{total}} \sum_{u=1}^{U} \sum_{m=1}^{M} B_m \log_2(1 + \frac{\sum\limits_{n \in \Omega_n} P_{u,n}}{N_s + \sum\limits_{n' \in \Omega_{n'}} P_{u,n'}}), \quad \Omega_n, \Omega_{n'} \subseteq [1, N]. \tag{4}$$

4   Optimal Solution

The exhaustive search is a common method of finding the optimal results [5], [16]. The basic idea of this algorithm is to try all the possible values within the whole variable fields and to generate all the possible objective results. Then, the value of the variable giving the best objective result is considered as the optimum. Therefore, the exhaustive search can guarantee the optimal results while it carries a large computational cost.

4.1   Implementation

As shown in (4), there are three variables for this resource block scheduling problem: which user (u), which resource block (m) and which base station (n). Based on the explanation of the investigated network in section 2.1, each RB can only be used once by each BS and the frequency reuse is flexible, so each RB can be used at most N times. Thus, there are NM resource block positions available for scheduling to at most U users, which can be represented as a 1 x NM scheduling vector to show the RB allocation case. Each element of the 1 x NM vector can be allocated to either none or one user in the network. Therefore, the number of the total possible combinations is $(U+1)^{NM}$.

4.2   Simulation Results and Analysis

The simulation results are for a 3-cell layout with one user per cell and three resource blocks in total. Even in this small network, the number of the total possible combinations is 4^9. For a more realistic problem with larger numbers of BSs, users and RBs, the exhaustive search becomes computationally unfeasible.

Inspection of the simulation results of the exhaustive search for this 3-cell network layout reveals that there are three types of RB allocation cases for the investigated network that may be optimal: full cooperation transmission, 2/3 reuse non-cooperative transmission and reuse 1 non-cooperative transmission. Full cooperation transmission means that all the resource blocks from all the base stations are scheduled to the same user (all the elements of the scheduling vector are scheduled to the same user), and this case occurs when the scheduled user has comparably good channel conditions to all the base stations while the other users have bad channel conditions to all the base stations; 2/3 reuse non-cooperative transmission means that all the resource blocks are used by 2/3 of the base stations (2/3 of the elements of the scheduling vector are scheduled), and this case occurs when the user in the base station not transmitting have a bad channel condition to its own base station but can cause considerable interference to the other users if resource blocks are scheduled to this user; reuse 1 non-cooperative transmission means that all the resource blocks from each base station are scheduled to its own user, and this case occurs when the users have good channel conditions to their own base stations while they have bad channel conditions to the other base stations in the layout.

5   Genetic Algorithm

Although the exhaustive search is able to give the optimal results, it requires a large amount of computation especially when the investigated network contains many users and many resource blocks. The Genetic Algorithm (GA) is also a search method which treats the variable as a chromosome [11], [15]. The chromosome (variable) will get genetic changes, e.g., crossover and mutation, and be measured by a fitness function until it meets the termination conditions which are normally used to control the precision of the outcomes.

5.1   Implementation

The process of the genetic algorithm is that a generation of individuals (chromosomes) get measured by a fitness function and the result from the fitness function is judged by the Termination Conditions (TC): if current result can satisfy the termination conditions, the solution is the current chromosome; if current result can not satisfy the termination conditions, the current generation of individuals will be genetically changed and the next generation of individuals will be generated and be measured by the fitness function and checked again. This process repeats until the result can meet the termination conditions. The details of the genetic algorithm can be found in [11,12,13]. There are four key parameters used in the genetic algorithm:

- Po: population size, more individuals used in a generation causes more computation but gives better results in the genetic algorithm.
- Re: replacement rate, the bad individuals will be replaced by the newly generated individuals.
- Co: crossover rate, one point crossover is used in this paper.
- Mu: mutation rate, a gene of an individual to be mutated is randomly selected, and the value of the selected gene will be changed.

This paper investigates the resource block scheduling in a cellular network to get as much total bandwidth efficiency as possible, and the optimal results have been obtained by the exhaustive search. Thus, the genetic algorithm is implemented in the same deployment as that used in the exhaustive search. The chromosome (variable) is the 1 x NM scheduling vector, of which each element is filled with none or one of the users whose locations are the same as those used by the exhaustive search. The fitness function is the total bandwidth efficiency calculated by (3). The selection of termination conditions for the genetic algorithm will be explained in section 5.2 and section 5.3.

5.2   Validation of the Genetic Algorithm

The first step is to check whether the genetic algorithm can be used to optimize total bandwidth efficiency by scheduling resource blocks.

The termination condition for validating the genetic algorithm should be based on the optimal results from the exhaustive search. Thus, the termination condition is selected to be the difference between the optimal results and the results from the genetic algorithm. The fitness function gives the results from the genetic algorithm, and then the difference from the optimal results can be computed. This difference will be compared with the constraint set in the termination condition to determine whether the optimal resource block allocation has been found by the genetic algorithm or more generations of individuals are needed.

The detailed simulation results are displayed and discussed in section 6.1. The conclusion can be drawn that the genetic algorithm is able to solve the scheduling problem to get optimal bandwidth efficiency.

5.3   Validation of the New Termination Conditions

The results for validating the genetic algorithm are based on the termination condition that requires the optimal results from the exhaustive search. Hence, new termination conditions without knowing the optimal results should be produced for the genetic algorithm to be applied to any network.

The termination condition in section 5.2 sets a constraint on the bandwidth efficiency difference to control the precision of the results from the genetic algorithm, so the new termination condition for any network also uses a constraint on the bandwidth efficiency difference between the current result and the maximal value of the previous results. Therefore, the search stops when the bandwidth efficiency difference between the current result and the maximal previous result is within a small value. Moreover, the minimum generation number for each search is also included in the new termination conditions. This avoids a situation that the search stops at a local optimum.

6   Simulation Results

In this section, the simulation results and the computation for validating the genetic algorithm will be displayed in section 6.1. The simulation results and the computation for validating new termination conditions will be discussed in section 6.2. Three aspects will be compared between the exhaustive search and the genetic algorithm: total bandwidth efficiency, selected resource block allocation case and computation. Total bandwidth efficiency will be shown as "Total bandwidth efficiency ratio" which is the ratio of the total bandwidth efficiency from the GA divided by the total bandwidth efficiency from the exhaustive search. Selected resource block allocation case will be displays as "Correct RB allocation" which is the percentage of the same RB allocation cases selected by the GA as those selected by the exhaustive search. Computation means the number of resource block scheduling combinations searched by the two algorithms. Computation of the GA relates to the population size and the generation number. "Averaged generation number" means the generation number in average in the simulation, and the computation of the GA can be calculated approximately by "Averaged generation number" times the population size [16].

All the simulation results are obtained for a 3-cell layout with one user per cell and three resource blocks in total. 1000 random independent user drops (1 user in each cell per drop) are generated as the user location samples.

6.1   Simulation Results of Validating the Genetic Algorithm

Table 2 displays the parameters of the genetic algorithm in this simulation. These parameters been selected following extensive experimentation to identify their impact upon the GA performance. The termination condition used in this simulation is that the bandwidth efficiency difference between the optimal result and the GA result is less than 10^{-1} bps/Hz.

Fig. 1 shows the CDF curves of the total bandwidth efficiency from three different algorithms: reuse 1 non-cooperation (users get all the resource blocks from their own BSs), the optimum (results from the exhaustive search) and the GA. From Fig. 1, both the GA and the optimum always outperform the reuse 1 non-cooperation, and the GA curve is almost the same as that of the optimum. Thus, the results from the GA are very close to those optimal results from the exhaustive search.

Table 3 gives the details of the comparison between the exhaustive search and the GA. Although the GA correctly selects 81.8% resource block allocation cases, the total bandwidth efficiency ratio is 99.98%. This implies that in the cases where the

Table 2. Parameters 1

Parameter	Value
Po	100
Co	0.4
Mu	0.01
Re	0.5

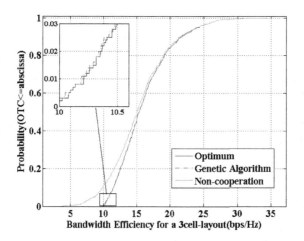

Fig. 1. Comparison of the CDF curves for validating GA

GA makes a non-optimal selection, the selection is nevertheless very close to the optimal one in terms of the bandwidth efficiency obtained. The purpose of using the GA is to achieve a total bandwidth efficiency as close as possible to the optimum, so this result shows that the genetic algorithm is validated for finding the optimal solution of the resource block scheduling problem. Moreover, the computation used in the GA is 2150 (Averaged generation number times the value of Po) while the computation used in the exhaustive search is 4^9 (all the possible combinations for the investigated network), so the GA only uses 0.82% of the computation required by the exhaustive search. Therefore, the GA can significantly reduce the computation compared with the exhaustive search even in this very small size problem.

Table 3. Simulation Results for Validating GA

Parameter	Value
Averaged generation number	21.4960
Correct RB allocation	81.80%
Total bandwidth efficiency ratio	99.98%

Fig. 2 shows the distribution of the generation number in the simulation. From Fig. 2, the curve tends to be flat after the generation number is 50, and 95.5% of the user drops can get results of the resource block allocation from the genetic algorithm by using no more than 50 generations. Thus, 50 is set as the minimum generation number in the new termination conditions for any network so that the search of the genetic algorithm after 50 generations is based on a near-optimal result for most of the users in a network without knowing the optimum. Fig. 2 however also shows that there are a small percentage of cases (around 4.5%) which have to use a larger number of generations to obtain a near optimum solution. This indicates that constraining the maximum generation number can constrain the computational requirement but at the

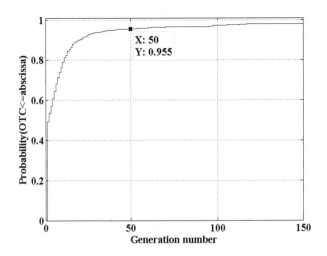

Fig. 2. The CDF distribution of the generation number

cost of optimality. Thus, the balance of the optimality and computation achieved by the genetic algorithm is a subject for further investigation, which is out of this paper but might be done in the future.

6.2   Simulation Results to Validate the Termination Conditions When the Optimum Results are Unknown

Whilst it is useful to show that the GA can achieve near-optimum performance by comparing with the exhaustive search, this is only possible for a small size problem, due to the excessive computation of the exhaustive search in larger problems. For larger problems, it is thus necessary to identify suitable termination conditions for the GA which do not rely on knowledge of the optimum.

Table 4 shows the parameters of the genetic algorithm used in this simulation. These have been modified based upon experimental observation to accommodate the change of termination conditions. The termination conditions for this simulation are that the bandwidth efficiency difference between the current result and the maximal previous result is less than 10^{-6} bps/Hz and each search must use no less than 50 generations.

Table 4. Parameters 2

Parameter	Value
Po	1200
Co	0.6
Mu	0.01
Re	0.4

Fig. 3 displays the three CDF curves of the total bandwidth efficiency from reuse 1 non-cooperation, the optimum and the GA. In Fig. 3, the curves of the optimum and the GA are almost identical which indicates that the results from the GA are still very close to those from the exhaustive search even when the termination conditions do not rely on knowledge of the optimum. Moreover, the curves of both the optimum and the GA are always superior to that of the reuse 1 non-cooperation.

From Table 5, 98.2% of the RB allocations made by the GA are optimal and the to-tal bandwidth efficiency ratio is approximately 100%. This shows that even those 1.8% non-optimal RB allocation cases selected by the GA can give excellent band-width efficiency results. Moreover, the averaged generation number is 51.872, which is very close to the minimum generation number of 50, and the number of the individ-uals used for each generation is 1200 (population size), so the computation of the GA is around 62247. The exhaustive search needs to calculate all possible RB allocation combinations which is 4^9. Thus, the genetic algorithm requires only 23.75% computa-tion of that of the exhaustive search and still can get approximately 100% optimal total bandwidth efficiency. Therefore, the modified termination conditions for any network in the GA are validated. Additionally, comparing with the results in section 6.1, it can be seen that the termination condition and the population size can have a

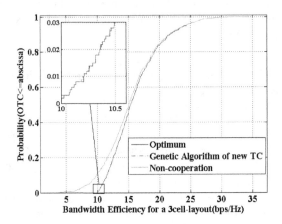

Fig. 3. Comparison of the CDF curves for validating the new TC

Table 5. Simulation Results of the New TC

Parameter	Value
Averaged generation number	51.8720
Correct RB allocation	98.20%
Total bandwidth efficiency ratio	100.00%

considerable influence on the results and the computation required: when larger population size is used or a minimal generation number is set in the termination condition, the results from the genetic algorithm are better while the computation required by the genetic algorithm is increased.

7   Conclusion

This paper has shown that the genetic algorithm can be used for finding a near-optimal resource block allocation solution for maximizing total bandwidth efficiency in a cooperative 3-cell network. The exhaustive search has been applied to a 3-cell network layout for the simulation to guarantee the optimal solution in the investigated network and a scheduling vector was used for representing the resource block allocation cases. Then, the genetic algorithm has been implemented in the same network layout and the same user locations to get results for the comparison with those from the exhaustive search. Firstly, the genetic algorithm has been validated by the termination condition relating to the optimal results from the exhaustive search. As a result, the termination condition has been modified and verified so that the genetic algorithm can be implemented in any network due to that the modified termination conditions no longer being based on the results from the exhaustive search. From the simulation results obtained, the genetic algorithm is capable of achieving a near-optimal resource block solution for maximizing total bandwidth efficiency. Moreover, the genetic algorithm can significantly reduce the computation required by the exhaustive search in the investigated network. Additionally, the population size and the termination condition can impact the results from the genetic algorithm and the computation that the genetic algorithm needs. Work to evaluate the performance of the genetic algorithm in a larger size network (with many users and many resource blocks) and to find solutions with lower complexity is now underway.

Acknowledgment. Zihan Luo wishes to thank her colleagues in the Communication Systems and Networks Laboratory for the many valuable discussions on aspects of this work.

References

1. Gesbert, D., Kiani, S.G., Gjendemsio, A., Ien, G.E.: Adaptation, coordination, and distributed resource allocation in interference-limited wireless networks. Proc. IEEE ISWCS **95**(12), 2393–2409 (2007)
2. Gesbert, D., Hanly, S., Huang, H., Shamai Shitz, S., Simeone, O., Yu, W.: Multi-cell MIMO cooperative networks: a new look at interference. IEEE Journal on Selected Areas in Communications **38**(9), 1380–1408 (2010)
3. Bhaskaran, S.R., Hanly, S.V., Badruddin, N., Evans, J.S.: Maximizing the sum rate in symmetric networks of interfering links. IEEE Transactions on Information Theory **56**(9), 4471–4487 (2010)
4. Gjendemsjoe, A., Gesbert, D., Oien, G., Kiani, S.: Binary power control for sum rate maximization over multiple interfering links. IEEE Trans. Wireless Commun. **7**(8), 3164–3173 (2008)
5. Issariyakul, T., Hossain, E.: Optimal radio channel allocation for fair queuing in wireless data networks. IEEE International Conference on Communications (ICC) **1**, 142–146 (2003)
6. Chang, R.Y., Tao, Z., Zhang, J., Kuo, C.-C.J.: Multicell OFDMA downlink resource allocation using a graphic framework. IEEE Transactions on Vehicular Technology **58**(7), 3494–3507 (2009)
7. Hou, I., Chen, C.S.: Self-organized resource allocation in LTE systems with weighted proportional fairness. In: IEEE international Conference on Communications (ICC 2012), pp. 5348–5353, June 2012
8. Ahn, W., Kim, Y.: An efficient resource-allocation scheme using subcarrier sharing in MIMO OFDM multi-cell environment. In: 14th Asia-Pacific Conference on Communications (APCC 2008), pp. 1–5, October 2008
9. Khun, H.W.: The Hungarian method for the assignment problem. Naval Research Logistics Quarterly **Q.2**, 83–97 (1995). http://tom.host.cs.st-andrews.ac.uk/CS3052-CC/Practicals/Kuhn.pdf
10. LTE; Evolved universal terrestrial radio access (E-UTRA); Radio frequency (RF) requirements for LTE Pico Node B (Release 9), 3GPP TR 36.931, May 2011
11. Li, G., Wu, J., Wang, G., Yu, H., Ma, G.: A new resource constrained scheduling method based on dynamic combination of genetic algorithm and ant algorithm. In: ASICON, pp. 1182–1185, October 2007
12. Wei, Y., Tian, L.: Research on cloud design resources scheduling based on genetic algorithm. In: International Conference on Systems and Informatics (ICSAI), pp. 2651–2656, May 2012

13. Yu, T., Zhao, K., Xu, F., Du, J., Wang, W.: Optimal scheduling of resources based on fuzzy set and genetic algorithm. In: WiCOM, pp. 1–4, October 2008
14. Patra, S., Roy, K., Banerjee, S., Vidyarthi, D.: Improved genetic algorithm for channel allocation with channel borrowing in mobile computing. IEEE Transactions on Mobile Computing **5**(7), 884–892 (2006)
15. Kalil, M., Samarabandu, J., Shami, A., Al-Dweik, A.: Performance evaluation of genetic algorithms for resource scheduling in LTE uplink. In: Wireless Communications and Mobile Computing Conference (IWCMC), pp. 948–952, August 2014
16. Elliott, R., Krzymien, W.: Downlink scheduling via genetic algorithms for multiuser single-carrier and multicarrier MIMO systems with dirty paper coding. IEEE Transactions on Vehicular Technology **58**(7), September 2009

Optimal and Equilibrium Retrial Rates in Single-Server Multi-orbit Retrial Systems

Konstantin Avrachenkov[1], Evsey Morozov[2], and Ruslana Nekrasova[2(✉)]

[1] Inria Sophia Antipolis, Valbonne, France
`K.Avrachenkov@sophia.inria.fr`
[2] Institute of Applied Mathematical Research,
Karelian Research Centre RAS, PetrSU, Petrozavodsk, Russia
`emorozov@karelia.ru, ruslana.nekrasova@mail.ru`

Abstract. We consider a single-server retrial system with one and several classes of customers. In the case of several classes, each class has its own orbit for retrying customers. The retrials from the orbits are generated with constant retrial rates. In the single class case, we are interested in finding an optimal retrial rate. Whereas in the multi-class case, we use game theoretic framework and find equilibrium retrial rates. Our performance criteria balance the number of retrials per retrying customer with the number of unhappy customers.

Keywords: Retrial queueing system · Constant retrial rate · Optimal retrial rate · Stability region · Multi-class system

1 Introduction

We study the optimization of the retrial rate in retrial systems with constant retrial rate and possibly several classes of customers. More specifically, we consider a retrial queueing system consisting of a service facility with only one server and no waiting space, and one or several orbits for retrying customers. If more than one class of customers exist in the system, each class has its own orbit. We consider a so-called constant retrial rate when the rate of retrials does not depend on the number of customers in orbit. We also consider an auxiliary case of the single class with additional exogenous input of non-retrying customers.

As a performance measure, we choose a linear combination of the expected number of unsuccessful attempts of a generic orbit customer and the expected number of jobs in orbit. In the single-class case, we obtain an explicit expression for the optimal retrial rate. In the multi-class case, we formulate the problem of choosing retrial rate in the game theoretic framework and, using a balance-rate argument, obtain an explicit approximation which performs very well. Furthermore, if there are just two classes and one class exhibit non-stable behaviour, the approximation becomes exact for the class with stable behaviour.

The retrial queueing systems with constant retrial rate has several applications. In [15] the retrial systems with constant retrial rate have been introduced

© Springer International Publishing Switzerland 2015
M. Jonsson et al. (Eds.): MACOM 2015, LNCS 9305, pp. 135–146, 2015.
DOI: 10.1007/978-3-319-23440-3_11

and applied to telephone exchange centers. The model of [15] was extended in [1], [2] for more complex settings, such as multiple servers and waiting places. Retrial systems under consideration can be applied to model ALOHA-type multiple access systems, see e.g., [10], [11], [18]. TCP transfers have been modelled by constant retrial rate queues in [8] and [9]. We expect that the analytical results of the present work will help to tune the retransmission rate in the ALOHA-type systems and the value of the retransmission timeout in TCP. The retrial systems with constant retrial rate have also been applied to model logistic systems [20].

The optimization and game theoretic problems in retrial queues have been studied, e.g., in [12–14,16,17,19,22]. In all papers, except [19], the system has only single class of customers and the decision makers are individual customers. In [19] a retrial system with two classes is analyzed. However, in [19] each customer retries independently and hence the rate of retrials grows with the number of orbit customers. In [12,22], the retrial rate is constant, but each customer takes his own decision and the decision consists in entering the system or reneging. Also, the objective function proposed in this work has not been analysed in the past.

The main contributions of this work are: explicit expressions for the optimal retrial rate in the single-class model and in the auxiliary model with exogenous input, and accurate approximation of the equilibrium retrial rates in the multiclass case. In fact, in the case of two classes, when one class is unstable, the proposed approximation becomes exact and provides best reply action for the stable class.

The paper is organized as follows: in the next section the models are formally presented. Then, in Section 3, the auxiliary model (with an exogenous input) is thoroughly investigated. In Section 4 we introduce multi-class retrial system with constant retrial rate and illustrate its connection with the auxiliary system. In Section 5, extensive numerical results are presented and discussed. We conclude the paper with Section 6.

2   Setting

We consider a single-server bufferless retrial queueing system with K classes of customers where class-i customers follow a Poisson arrival process with rate λ_i, have i.i.d. exponential service times with rate μ_i and, provided the server is busy upon arrival, join orbit $i = 1, \ldots, K$. Orbit i works like a single-server queueing system with (exponential) constant rate retrial time (with rate α_i) regardless of the orbit size. Thus, there are K different orbits with retrial customers, and the ith orbit behaves like the orbit of a single-class system. We denote this original system by Σ.

Also consider the following auxiliary retrial system $\tilde{\Sigma}$ with two Poisson inputs with rates λ (input 1) and λ_0 (input 2), respectively. The blocked customers from input 1 join an orbit and then attempt to enter server after the exponentially distributed retrial time with rate α, while the blocked customers from input 2 leave the system forever. The system has the exponentially distributed service times with rate μ. Denote by $\tilde{N}$ the stationary orbit size in system $\tilde{\Sigma}$ (if exists) and by $\tilde{\gamma}$ the number of the unsuccessful attempts which a blocked customer makes in stationary regime of system $\tilde{\Sigma}$ before a successful attempt. In this work, we will solve the following optimization problem: select a value of retrial rate α (denoted hereafter α^*) in system $\tilde{\Sigma}$ which, for fixed parameters λ, λ_0, μ, provides the minimum of function

$$\tilde{F}(\alpha) := c_1 E\tilde{\gamma} + c_2 E\tilde{N}, \tag{1}$$

where c_i are some positive constants.

The motivation for such a choice of penalty function (1) is as follows. On the one hand, we do not want to create too many requests for service (e.g., avoiding Denial of Service attack). This corresponds to minimization of $E\tilde{\gamma}$. On the other hand, we would like to keep as few as possible customers in unhappy situation. This corresponds to minimization of $E\tilde{N}$. This motivation is supported below by explicit expressions (8) and (10) which show that indeed $E\tilde{\gamma}$ increases and $E\tilde{N}$ decreases, as α increases.

Denote by N, γ the corresponding parameters in the system Σ, related to the 1st class customers, and consider a function

$$F(\alpha_1) := c_1 E\gamma + c_2 EN, \tag{2}$$

where α_1 is the retrial rate of the 1st class customers. Note that we have no explicit formula for F, and only rely on approximation and simulation. On the other hand, the system $\tilde{\Sigma}$ is less complicated (than original multi-class system Σ), and in section 3 we present an explicit expression for function $\tilde{F}$. In spite of the difference between the models Σ and $\tilde{\Sigma}$, we will show that the analysis of a simpler model $\tilde{\Sigma}$ allows to select a near-optimal value of the retrial rate in the system Σ, which provides the value of function F close to the minimum. We note that in the multi-class multi-orbit case, we consider the performance optimization from the game theoretic viewpoint.

3   Analysis of the Auxiliary System

We consider the two-dimensional process $\{X(t) := (\tilde{M}(t), \tilde{N}(t)), t \geq 0\}$, where $\tilde{M}(t)$ is the number of customers in the server (that is $\tilde{M}(t) \in \{0, 1\}$), and $\tilde{N}(t)$ is the number of customers in orbit, at instant t, in system $\tilde{\Sigma}$. We use notation P_{mn} for the corresponding stationary probabilities of the process $\{X(t)\}$ (so $m = 0$, 1 and $n \geq 0$). A close model has been recently analyzed in paper [12]. To adapt below some required results from [12] to our model, we first show an equivalence between our model and the model from [12]. Authors in [12] present a retrial queueing system with Poisson input with a rate λ. Customers enter a retrial queue (orbit) with probability r whenever the server is busy and with probability 1 whenever the server is idle. The time required to find a costumer from the retrial orbit is assumed exponentially distributed with rate α. Now we show that this model is indeed equivalent to the model $\tilde{\Sigma}$ with extra input.

The retrial rate α in [12] is the same as α in system $\tilde{\Sigma}$, the input rate λ (in [12]) is replaced in our model by $\lambda + \lambda_0$. If a customer from an extra input (with rate λ_0) in system $\tilde{\Sigma}$ faces a busy server we detect a loss. Thus, if server is busy, an arrival from the input (with rate $\lambda + \lambda_0$) is lost with the probability $\lambda_0/(\lambda + \lambda_0)$ which is probability r in [12]. From this point of view, both systems are equivalent.

Returning to our system $\tilde{\Sigma}$, denote as P_1 and P_0 stationary probabilities of busy and idle server, respectively. The explicit values for P_1 and P_0 could easily be obtained after some calculation using Kolmogorov's equations technique and generation function method. Note that balance equations for stationary probabilities in considered system is equivalent to equations in [12] (see (3.7) – (3.9) there). The idle and busy probabilities have the following form:

$$P_0 = \frac{\mu - \lambda}{\mu + \lambda_0}, \tag{3}$$

$$P_1 = \frac{\lambda + \lambda_0}{\mu + \lambda_0}, \tag{4}$$

which is equivalent to (3.3), (3.4) in [12]. Using also Kolmogorov's equations technique, it is rather easy to get the formula for the probability of empty system as follows:

$$P_{00} = P_0 - \frac{\lambda}{\alpha} P_1. \tag{5}$$

Note that P_1 is the busy probability which (by PASTA property) is also the blocking probability of an arriving primary customer. It follows from (3)-(5) that

$$P_{00} = 1 - \frac{(\lambda + \lambda_0)}{(\mu + \lambda_0)} - \frac{\lambda}{\alpha} \cdot \frac{(\lambda + \lambda_0)}{(\mu + \lambda_0)}. \tag{6}$$

It is easy to check by (3), (4) that

$$P_1 = \frac{\lambda + \lambda_0 P_0}{\mu}. \tag{7}$$

To explain (7), we note that the the effective input rate in the stationary system $\tilde{\Sigma}$ (that is the limiting time-average rate of the customers entering the server) is $\lambda_e := \lambda + \lambda_0 P_0$, and it is well-known that then the stationary busy probability of the server equals $P_1 = \lambda_e/\mu$. The mean orbit size can be expressed in the following form (for detail see statement (3.13) in [12], and also [3],[7]):

$$E\tilde{N} = \frac{\lambda(\lambda + \lambda_0)(\lambda + \lambda_0 + \mu + \alpha)}{\mu(\mu + \lambda_0)(\alpha - \rho(\lambda + \lambda_0 + \alpha))}, \tag{8}$$

where $\rho := \lambda/\mu$.

With no loss of generality, we assume that each blocked primary costumer joins the end of the orbit queue, and only head (top) customer in the orbit queue attempts to enter server until success. Denote $\tilde{\gamma}_n$ the total number of the unsuccessful attempts of the nth retrying customer. Then variables $\{\tilde{\gamma}_n, n \geq 1\}$

constitute an i.i.d. sequence (with generic element $\tilde{\gamma}$). If a customer completes service, then a primary customer occupies server with the probability

$$p := \int_0^\infty (\lambda + \lambda_0) e^{-(\lambda + \lambda_0) x} e^{-\alpha x} dx = \frac{\lambda + \lambda_0}{\lambda + \lambda_0 + \alpha}, \tag{9}$$

and thus p is the probability of the unsuccessful attempt of the head orbital customer to capture free server after a departure. Note that the average number of (certainly) unsuccessful attempts during service time is equal to

$$\int_0^\infty \sum_{k=0}^\infty k \frac{(\alpha x)^k}{k!} e^{-\alpha x} \mu e^{-\mu x} dx = \frac{\alpha}{\mu}.$$

Now assume that there is only (top) orbital customer. Then he attempts to access the server after joining orbit, and thus the average number of the unsuccessful attempts during service time is α/μ. Otherwise, assume a few orbital customers, and a customer, already being in orbit, becomes top after starting service (of an orbital customer). Again the average number of his unsuccessful attempts during service time is α/μ. Thus, anyway $E\tilde{\gamma} \geq \alpha/\mu$. Then each new unsuccessful attempt to capture empty server after a departure gives on average α/μ unsuccessful attempts (of the top orbital customer) during next service time. This immediately yields the following expression

$$E\tilde{\gamma} = \frac{\alpha}{\mu} + \frac{\alpha}{\mu} \cdot \sum_{k=1}^\infty p^k = \frac{\lambda + \lambda_0 + \alpha}{\mu}. \tag{10}$$

Now we obtain from (8), (10) (also see (1)) that

$$\tilde{F}(\alpha) = c_1 \cdot \frac{\lambda + \lambda_0 + \alpha}{\mu} + c_2 \cdot \frac{\lambda(\lambda + \lambda_0)(\lambda + \lambda_0 + \mu + \alpha)}{\mu(\mu + \lambda_0)(\alpha - \rho(\lambda + \lambda_0 + \alpha))}. \tag{11}$$

Next one can check that

$$\frac{d(E\tilde{N})}{d\alpha} = \frac{-\rho(\lambda + \lambda_0)}{(\alpha(1 - \rho) - \rho(\lambda + \lambda_0))^2}, \tag{12}$$

implying

$$\frac{d\tilde{F}}{d\alpha} = \frac{c_1}{\mu} - \frac{c_2 \lambda(\lambda + \lambda_0)}{\mu(\alpha - \rho(\lambda + \lambda_0 + \alpha))^2}. \tag{13}$$

Then, after some algebra, equation $\tilde{F}'(\alpha) = 0$ gives the following explicit expression for the optimizer:

$$\alpha^* = \frac{\mu\sqrt{c_2/c_1}\sqrt{\lambda(\lambda + \lambda_0)} + \lambda(\lambda + \lambda_0)}{\mu - \lambda}. \tag{14}$$

In particular, if we set $\lambda_0 = 0$, we obtain a nice explicit expression for the optimal value of the retrial rate in the single-class model:

$$\alpha^* = \lambda \frac{\mu\sqrt{c_2/c_1} + \lambda}{\mu - \lambda}. \tag{15}$$

To the best of our knowledge, this is a new result.

To guarantee α^* to be well-defined, we must define stability condition. It is shown in [12] (Proposition 3.1) that the system $\tilde{\Sigma}$ is stable if and only if

$$\rho(\lambda + \lambda_0 + \alpha) < \alpha. \tag{16}$$

By the noted above equivalence of the systems, it is also stability criteria of the original system Σ. Note that (16) can be written as

$$\rho < 1 - p, \tag{17}$$

where p is defined in (9) and implies that $\rho < 1$. Also we note that for $\lambda_0 = 0$ condition (16) coincides with stability criterion of the single-orbit retrial M/M/1-type system obtained in [4]. (We remark that stability analysis of the retrial system with constant retrial rate is also presented in [3], [21].)

4   Multi-class Multi-orbit System

In this section we discuss the relations between original K-orbit system and the auxiliary two-class system $\tilde{\Sigma}$. In particular we show how to apply to original system the analytical results obtained for the auxiliary system $\tilde{\Sigma}$. The key link connecting both systems (provided that *all orbits in Σ are stable*) is the following balance relation between the *effective input rate* $\lambda_0 P_0$ in the system $\tilde{\Sigma}$ and given input rates λ_i, $i = 2, \cdots, K$ in the system Σ:

$$\lambda_0 P_0 = \sum_{i=2}^{K} \lambda_i. \tag{18}$$

It establishes a balance between the total workload arriving in both systems and implies the equality of limiting fractions of the server busy times in both systems. In turn, it implies the equality of the stationary busy probabilities in both systems. However, the effective input of λ_0-customers (entering the server) in the system $\tilde{\Sigma}$ is a result of a (state-depending) thinning of the λ_0-input, while, in the system Σ, the inter-arrival times of the i-th class customers finally entering server are a complicated combination of the original (exponential) interarrival times and a random sum of the retrial times between the unsuccessful attempts until a successful attempt occurs. It is remarkable that, in spite of this difference between the two systems, the optimal value α^* found analytically for the system $\tilde{\Sigma}$ allows to approximate the required optimal retrial rate in the system Σ with a high precision, see Section 5. It is important to stress that the inputs of class-i customers with $i \geq 2$, from the point of view of class-1 customers, can be considered as a single Poisson input with the summary rate $\lambda_0 P_0$. Thus, the analysis of original K-orbit system with arbitrary K is reduced to the analysis of the auxiliary system $\tilde{\Sigma}$. Note that the stability conditions found in [5,6] allow to select the corresponding parameters in such a way that the 1st class orbits in both systems are always stable, while the 2nd class orbit in system Σ may be either stable or unstable. Now we focus on two-orbit system Σ and recall that the 1-class orbit in the system Σ is assumed to be stable. Thus, we will distinguish the following possible cases.

The 2nd Stable Orbit: Symmetric Case. Assume that two classes are equivalent with the same input rate $\lambda_1 = \lambda_2 := \lambda$, the same service rate $\mu_1 = \mu_2 = \mu$ and the same retrial rate $\alpha_1 = \alpha_2 := \alpha$. Then the 2nd orbit (in system Σ) is stable, and the input of the 2nd class of customers is interpreted as λ_0-input in system $\tilde{\Sigma}$. For this symmetric case balance equation (18) becomes

$$\lambda_0 P_0 = \lambda. \tag{19}$$

Then it follows from (3) that

$$\lambda_0 = \frac{\mu\lambda}{\mu - 2\lambda}, \tag{20}$$

and (14) gives us

$$\alpha^* = \sqrt{\lambda\left(\lambda + \frac{\mu\lambda}{\mu - 2\lambda}\right)} \cdot \frac{\left(\sqrt{c_2/c_1} \cdot \mu + \sqrt{\lambda[\lambda + \mu\lambda/(\mu - 2\lambda)]}\right)}{(\mu - \lambda)}. \tag{21}$$

The 2nd Stable Orbit: Non-symmetric Case. Consider the system Σ with non-equivalent classes, that is, $\lambda_1 \neq \lambda_2$, $\alpha_1 \neq \alpha_2$, and the same service rate μ for both classes. According to (18), $\lambda_0 = \lambda_2/P_0$, and we obtain (see (3))

$$\lambda_0 = \frac{\mu\lambda_2}{\mu - (\lambda_1 + \lambda_2)}. \tag{22}$$

Then (14) implies

$$\alpha^* = \sqrt{\lambda_1\left(\lambda_1 + \frac{\mu\lambda_2}{\mu - (\lambda_1 + \lambda_2)}\right)} \cdot \frac{\left(\sqrt{c_2/c_1} \cdot \mu + \sqrt{\lambda_1(\lambda_1 + \mu\lambda_2/[\mu - (\lambda_1 + \lambda_2)])}\right)}{(\mu - \lambda_1)}.$$

Our purpose is to find the optimal α_1 for the fixed α_2. Furthermore, we note that, by (22), λ_0 is independent of α_2. Thus, our approximation can be interpreted as equilibrium rate in game theoretic framework. It follows from [5,6] that the necessary stability conditions of original system are

$$\lambda_i P_b < (1 - P_b)\alpha_i, \quad i = 1, 2, \tag{23}$$

where $P_b := (\lambda_1 + \lambda_2)/\mu$ is the *busy probability*. We note that (23) is stability criteria in the symmetric case [5]. Thus, if the 2nd orbit in Σ is stable, then

$$\lambda_2 \frac{(\lambda_1 + \lambda_2)}{\mu} < \left(1 - \frac{\lambda_1 + \lambda_2}{\mu}\right)\alpha_2, \tag{24}$$

and the following *stability measure* of the 2nd orbit,

$$\Gamma_2 := \big(\mu - (\lambda_1 + \lambda_2)\big)\alpha_2 - \lambda_2(\lambda_1 + \lambda_2), \qquad (25)$$

is positive (whenever the 2nd orbit is stable). Moreover, as Γ_2 increases, the system Σ moves "deeper" in the stability region of the 2nd orbit.

The 2nd Unstable Orbit. Now assume that the 2nd orbit is unstable (with a fixed rate α_2). In this case the systems Σ, $\tilde{\Sigma}$ become identical for class-1 customers, and parameter λ_0 is defined as

$$\lambda_0 = \lambda_2 + \alpha_2, \qquad (26)$$

implying

$$\alpha^* = \sqrt{\lambda_1(\lambda_1 + \lambda_2 + \alpha_2)} \cdot \frac{\big(\sqrt{c_2/c_1} \cdot \mu + \sqrt{\lambda_1(\lambda_1 + \lambda_2 + \alpha_2)}\big)}{(\mu - \lambda_1)}. \qquad (27)$$

This gives the best reply of the 1st class for any action of the 2nd class. We note that since the 2nd orbit is unstable, the objective function of the 2nd class takes infinite value. Nevertheless, the objective function of the 1st class is well-defined and takes finite values. This is one more confirmation that the constant retrial rate can be protective [7].

Remark 1. The equivalence of both systems from the point of view of class-1 customers follows from discussion in the work [6] where more detailed analysis of unstable orbits can be found.

5   Simulation Results

In this section we compare analytical results for the auxiliary $\tilde{\Sigma}$ with the numerical results for the corresponding two-orbit system Σ. More exactly, we compare the objective function $\tilde{F}(\alpha)$ (see (1)) with the empirical function

$$\hat{F}(\alpha_1) = c_1\hat{\gamma} + c_2\hat{N}, \qquad (28)$$

where $\hat{\gamma}$, $\hat{N}$ are the sample means of the number of unsuccessful attempts and the 1st orbit size, respectively, in the original system Σ, based on 500 independent replications.

1. Consider *symmetric case*, then the 2nd orbit is stable as well. In Table 1, simulation results for $\lambda_1 = \lambda_2 = \lambda = 1$, and $\mu = 3$ are given. Note that α^* is obtained from (21), $\hat{\alpha}^*$ is the estimated retrial rate (for both orbits in the system Σ) which provides the minimum of function $\hat{F}$, and ε is the relative error of $\hat{\alpha}^*$.

As Table 1 shows, the best fit (the smallest relative error $\varepsilon = 3.9 \times 10^{-9}$) is obtained if $c_1/c_2 = 25$ (and $\mu = 3$). It means that a small number of the unsuccessful attempts and, as a result a rarity of attacks on server, is more

Table 1. Simulation results for symmetric Σ.

c_1/c_2	μ	α^*	$\hat{\alpha}^*$	ε	F	$\hat{F}$	λ_0
1	3	5.000	4.600	0.080	4.333	5.232	3.000
1	8	2.079	1.800	0.134	0.805	0.789	1.333
1	30	1.576	1.400	0.112	0.175	0.153	1.111
25	3	2.6000	2.600	0.000	60.333	62.821	3.000
25	8	0.682	0.600	0.121	10.551	10.671	1.333
25	30	0.369	0.400	0.083	2.284	2.306	1.111
1/25	3	17.000	15.600	0.082	20.333	31.396	3.000
1/25	8	9.062	6.800	0.25	3.408	3.322	1.333
1/25	30	7.516	5.200	0.202	0.625	0.455	1.111

important than a small orbit size. Moreover, as μ increases (from $\mu = 3$ to $\mu = 30$), then evidently, the system moves deeper into stability region and the relative error increases.

For all values of c_1/c_2 the smallest relative error is obtained for the most slow rate $\mu = 3$ because in this case the orbits are the most saturated, and the system Σ is better described by the analytical results obtained for the system $\tilde{\Sigma}$. Also we note that the worst results are obtained for $c_1/c_2 = 1/25$, in which case the orbit size is more important than the number of attempts. In the most of cases (except $c_1/c_2 = 25$, $\mu = 30$) the estimated optimal value $\hat{\alpha}^*$ satisfies

$$0.9 \cdot \alpha^* \leq \hat{\alpha}^* \leq \alpha^*. \tag{29}$$

This approximation can be used in practice to select a near optimal retrial rate in the original system, based on analytical result obtained for the system $\tilde{\Sigma}$. Figure 1 shows a difference between F and $\hat{F}$ (depending on α) for $c_1 = c_2 = 1$.

2. Consider *asymmetric case*. We take $\lambda_1 = \lambda_2 = 1$ and $\mu = 3$, implying $\lambda_0 = 3$ in the auxiliary system $\tilde{\Sigma}$. If classes are not equivalent, then we *assume* that the violation of conditions (23) for $i = 2$ implies instability of the 2nd orbit. (Note that this assumption is confirmed by simulation of all considered scenarios.) For

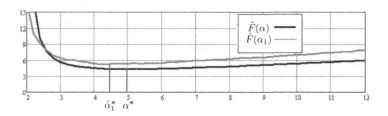

Fig. 1. $\tilde{F}(\alpha)$ vs. $\hat{F}(\alpha_1)$ for $c_1 = c_2 = 1$, $\mu = 3$, $\alpha^* = 5$, $\hat{\alpha}_1^* = 4.6$.

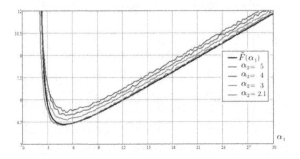

Fig. 2. $F(\alpha_1)$ vs. $\hat{F}(\alpha_1)$, $\lambda_1 = \lambda_2 = 1$, $\lambda_0 = 3$, $\mu = 3$.

fixed parameters $\lambda_1 = \lambda_2 = 1$, $\mu = 3$ and the values $\alpha_2 = 5, 4, 3, 2.1$, we obtain the following values of the stability measure $\Gamma_2 : 3, 2, 1, 0.1$, respectively. The positivity of Γ_2 implies the fulfilment of condition (23) and, consequently, stability of the system. Note that, for $\alpha_2 = 2.1$, the 2nd stable orbit is near the stability region border and empties very rarely. On Figure 2, functions $F(\alpha_1)$, $\hat{F}(\alpha_1)$ are presented for a few values of α_2. Note that α_1 also denotes the orbit rate in $\tilde{\Sigma}$. We investigate the behavior of $\hat{F}$ in system Σ for various α_1, having α_2 fixed and $\Gamma_2 > 0$.

The curves in Figure 2 become closer as the 2nd orbit becomes *less stable* (*more saturated*). For instance, if $\alpha_2 = 2.1$ (then $\Gamma_2 = 0.1$), then the curves almost coincide. This proximity becomes the equality when the 2nd orbit is unstable, as we show in the next point. (Also see *Remark 1* in Section 4.)

3. Finally, consider *asymmetric case with unstable 2nd orbit*. Thus, the value of α^* is given by (27). Figure 3 shows F and $\hat{F}$ with parameters $\lambda_1 = 0.3$, $\lambda_2 = 3$, $\mu = 4$, $\alpha_2 = 5$. In this case, the class-2 input is Poisson with rate $\lambda_2 + \alpha_2$ and, as a result, functions F and $\hat{F}$ coincide. Thus, if the 2nd orbit is unstable, the value $\alpha^* = 2.37$ *becomes optimal*, best response, for the 1st class customers in system Σ.

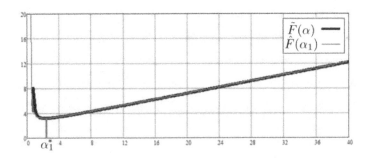

Fig. 3. $F(\alpha)$ vs. $\hat{F}(\alpha)$, $c_1 = c_2 = 1$, $\mu = 4$, $\alpha_1^* = 2.37$.

Remark 2. It is worth mentioning that, as simulation shows, the estimated (optimal) parameter $\hat{\alpha}^*$ in the systems with $K = 5$, 10, 20, 50 classes satisfies condition (29) as well.

6   Conclusion

For a Markovian multi-class single-server retrial system with constant retrial rates depending on class of customers, we find an optimal (equilibrium) retrial rate of a fixed class customers using optimization and game theoretic frameworks and a balance between the number of retrials (per customer) and the number of orbital customers. To address this problem, we study a more simple auxiliary system with exogenous Poisson input, which, in spite of the difference with the original system, allows to predict optimal retrial rate in the original system with a remarkable accuracy.

Acknowledgments. This work is supported by Russian Foundation for Basic research, projects Nos 15–07–02341, 15–07–02354, 15–07–02360, by the Program of strategic development of Petrozavodsk State University, and by EU COST ACROSS action No IC–1304.

References

1. Artalejo, J.R.: Stationary analysis of the characteristics of the M/M/2 queue with constant repeated attempts. Opsearch **33**, 83–95 (1996)
2. Artalejo, J.R., Gómez-Corral, A., Neuts, M.F.: Analysis of multiserver queues with constant retrial rate. European Journal of Operational Research **135**, 569–581 (2001)
3. Avrachenkov, K., Goricheva, R.S., Morozov, E.V.: Verification of stability region of a retrial queuing system by regenerative method. In: Proceedings of the International Conference "Modern Probabilistic Methods for Analysis and Optimization of Information and Telecommunication Networks", Minsk, pp. 22–28 (2011)
4. Avrachenkov, K., Morozov, E.V.: Stability analysis of $GI/G/c/K$ retrial queue with constant retrial rate. Math. Meth. Oper. Res. **79**, 273–291 (2014)
5. Avrachenkov, K., Morozov, E., Nekrasova, R., Steyaert, B.: Stability analysis of retrial systems with constant retrial rates. In: First European Conference on Queueing Theory, ECQT 2014, Booklet of Abstracts, p. 50 (2014)
6. Avrachenkov, K., Morozov, E., Nekrasova, R., Steyaert, B.: Stability analysis and simulation of N-class retrial system with constant retrial rates and Poisson inputs. Asia-Pacific Journal of Operational Research **31**(2), 18 (2014)
7. Avrachenkov, K., Nain, P., Yechiali, U.: A retrial system with two input streams and two orbit queues. Queueing Systems **77**(1), 1–31 (2014)
8. Avrachenkov, K., Yechiali, U.: Retrial networks with finite buffers and their application to Internet data traffic. Probability in the Engineering and Informational Sciences **22**, 519–536 (2008)
9. Avrachenkov, K., Yechiali, U.: On tandem blocking queues with a common retrial queue. Computers and Operations Research **37**(7), 1174–1180 (2010)

10. Choi, B.D., Rhee, K.H., Park, K.K.: The M/G/1 retrial queue with retrial rate control policy. Probability in the Engineering and Informational Sciences **7**, 29–46 (1993)
11. Choi, B.D., Shin, Y.W., Ahn, W.C.: Retrial queues with collision arising from unslotted CSMA/CD protocol. Queueing Systems **11**, 335–356 (1992)
12. Economou, A., Kanta, S.: Equilibrium customer strategies and social-profit maximization in the single-server constant retrial queue. Naval Research Logistics (NRL) **58**(2), 107–122 (2011)
13. Elcan, A.: Optimal customer return rate for an M/M/1 queueing system with retrials. Probability in the Engineering and Informational Sciences **8**(4), 5211–7539 (1994)
14. Elcan, A.: Asymptotic bounds for an optimal state-dependent retrial rate of the M/M/1 queue with returning customers. Mathematical and Computer Modelling **30**(31–74), 129–140 (1999)
15. Fayolle, G.: A simple telephone exchange with delayed feedback. In: Boxma, O.J., Cohen J.W., Tijms, H.C. (eds.) Teletraffic Analysis and Computer Performance Evaluation, vol. 7, pp. 245–253 (1986)
16. Hassin, R., Haviv, M.: On optimal and equilibrium retrial rates in a queueing system. Probability in the Engineering and Informational Sciences **10**(2), 2231–7227 (1996)
17. Hassin, R., Haviv, M.: To queue or not to queue: Equilibrium behavior in queueing systems. Springer (2003)
18. Kobliakov, V.A., Turlikov, A.M., Vinel, A.V.: Distributed queue random multiple access algorithm for centralized data networks. In: IEEE Tenth International Symposium on Consumer Electronics, ISCE 2006 (2006)
19. Kulkarni, V.G.: A game theoretic model for two types of customers competing for service. Operations Research Letters **2**(3), 1191–7122 (1983)
20. Lillo, R.E.: A G/M/1-queue with exponential retrial. TOP **4**(1), 99–120 (1996)
21. Morozov, E., Nekrasova, R.: Estimation of blocking probability in retrial queuing system with constant retrial rate. In: Proceedings of the Institute of Applied Mathematical Research, Karelian Research Centre RAS, vol. 5, pp. 63–74 (2011). (in Russian)
22. Zhang, Z., Wang, J., Zhang., F.: Equilibrium Customer Strategies in the Single-Server Constant Retrial Queue with Breakdowns and Repairs. Mathematical Problems in Engineering, 14 (2014)

GOAT: A Tool for Planning Wireless Sensor Networks

Sergio Barrachina, Toni Adame, Albert Bel, and Boris Bellalta[✉]

Department of Information and Communication Technologies,
Universitat Pompeu Fabra, Barcelona, Spain
sergio.barrachina01@estudiant.upf.edu,
{boris.bellalta,toni.adame,albert.bel}@upf.edu

Abstract. This paper presents GOAT, a software tool that has been developed to study the effect of different Medium Access Control (MAC) and routing protocols on the energy consumption in Wireless Sensor Networks (WSNs). GOAT is a graphical network analysis tool that allows designing WSNs, calculating the energy consumption and overall lifetime in thoroughly configurable WSN scenarios. The aim of the GOAT tool is to obtain a knowledge of the behaviour of WSNs in terms of nodes connectivity and energy consumption prior to the WSN deployment in a real environment.

1 Introduction

Wireless Sensor Networks (WSNs) are positioned to be one of the fastest growing communication fields in the next years. These networks are composed of tiny devices (nodes) used to gather environmental information, process it locally, and then communicate it via wireless links to a central coordinating node, known as sink. Due to the small size of nodes, energy capacity of batteries is also small; therefore reducing energy consumption is vital in these networks, since it is not always possible to replace or recharge them. Hence, the major goal in terms of energy efficiency is to maximize the lifetime of the network while still providing appropriate quality of service (QoS) requirements.

Regarding energy consumption, the Medium Access Control (MAC) layer protocol is crucial due to its influence on the sensor transceiver, which is the most energy-consuming component of a sensor node. Several MAC protocols such as B-MAC [1], X-MAC [2], LWT-MAC [3] or the power saving mechanisms implemented in IEEE 802.11ah [4] have been designed to reduce the energy consumption in WSNs. A general overview of MAC protocols for WSNs can be found in [5]. However, WSNs are usually application specific; therefore, the selection of the protocol stack, and specially the MAC layer, strongly depends on the network application and its topology. In order to ensure future proper performance and maximum lifetime of a certain WSN, it is recommended to perform different simulations and tests before implementing it in a real environment. Nonetheless, running real experiments on WSN testbeds is costly and challenging.

© Springer International Publishing Switzerland 2015
M. Jonsson et al. (Eds.): MACOM 2015, LNCS 9305, pp. 147–158, 2015.
DOI: 10.1007/978-3-319-23440-3_12

With GOAT [6], we provide a graphical network analyzer that allows designing and evaluating future real operating WSNs before building them, whose main outcomes are the WSN energy consumption and overall lifetime estimations in a huge variety of scenarios. This software aims to be as modular as possible in order to facilitate future open source collaborations to improve and extend the GOAT capabilities. GOAT implements several propagation, battery, MAC and routing models that can be selected by the user to build the scenarios of interest. GOAT has several features such as network topology representation, reading and saving topology data files, packet rates displaying, functional graphical user interface (GUI), and energy consumption estimation in a huge number of scenarios, among others.

As a proof of concept, this paper presents the analysis of a plague tracking WSN scenario based on the ENTOMATIC[1] project [7], where GOAT has been used to determine the WSN lifetime in multiple configurations depending on the number of nodes and the packet generation rate.

The remainder of this paper is organized as follows: In Section 2, the GOAT tool description and design are depicted. The GOAT modules used in the plague tracking use-case are presented in Section 3. Section 4 depicts the considered plague tracking use-case. The results obtained are presented in section 5. Finally, in Section 6, the conclusions can be found.

2   GOAT Tool

GOAT [6] is a graphical Wireless Sensor Network planning tool compatible with Windows, Mac OS and Linux operating systems (only Java JDK 7.0 or above is required). With GOAT, we provide a tool that allows WSN designers to evaluate the effects of different propagation models, MAC and network protocols in the network lifetime for a given topology and application requirements. Hence, they are able to select the most appropriate protocols for a given WSN use-case.

GOAT displays on the screen the topology of the planned network, i.e., nodes and links, and also informs about different parameters of interest such as packet transmission and reception rates, number of nodes and map size. All the mentioned graphical items are included in a Graphical User Interface (GUI) that enables interacting with the planner throughout a series of panels, buttons, combo boxes and checkboxes.

GOAT is aimed to be an open source project, so that, it has been designed taking into account code modularity for promoting future collaborations. The main goal is that GOAT could be used in educational, research and business fields, facilitating learning WSN aspects in the first case, allowing deeper analysis on the second one, and providing a fully functional planning tool in the third one.

---

[1] ENTOMATIC stands for *Novel automatic and stand-alone integrated pest management tool for remote count and bioacoustics identification of the Olive Fruit Fly (Bactrocera oleae) in the field.*

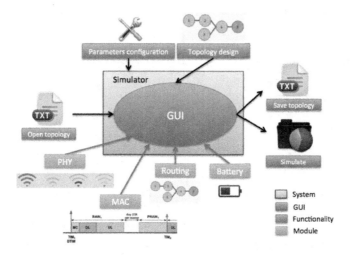

Fig. 1. GOAT functional design

2.1 Features

The main features implemented by GOAT are: creating and modifying WSN topologies, saving and opening topology files, set and modify the message sending rates for each node and the place of the sink, adding and deleting sensor nodes, displaying information about distance between nodes and received power, displaying coverage areas and routing links, estimating the energy consumption of each node and its lifetime depending on the modules selected, analyzing the selected battery model impact on the WSN energy consumption, estimating the proportion of the time a node stays in transmitting, receiving and sleeping states, and saving simulation results.

2.2 Functional Design

GOAT allows creating and modifying WSNs topologies through its GUI. Also, from the GUI, a user has the possibility to select different physical, battery, MAC, and routing models for modeling the desired scenario. In order to open stored topologies and save new ones, the GUI has buttons for reading input topologies files in .txt format and writing new ones. Simulations results are displayed on the console and can be stored in .csv format files. The functional design diagram is shown in Figure 1.

For this first version of GOAT, a minimalist GUI design has been proposed (see Figure 2), with few text and buttons placed in a recognizable interface, matching the usual patterns, commands and metaphors (e.g., play icon for simulating).

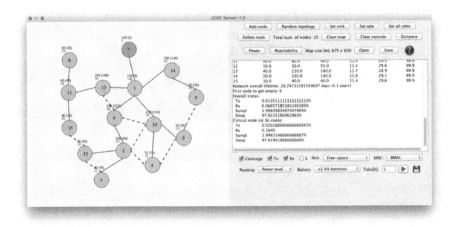

Fig. 2. GOAT GUI

2.3   Modules

The modules implemented in the first version of GOAT are shown in Table 1.

Table 1. Modules implemented in the first version of GOAT

Module	Model
PHY	Free-space path loss
	Log-normal path loss
MAC	B-MAC (and B-MAC/ACK)
	IEEE 802.11ah
Routing	Single-hop
	First-response
	Closest-node
Battery	2x AA (7,500 mAh)
	2x AAA (1,500 mAh)
	Lithium battery (2,200 mAh)

2.4   Areas of Improvement

Some of the main features that have been identified as major aspects of improvement are: configurating parameters from the GUI (avoid modifying hard-coded parameters), including packet collisions option for making the simulation results more accurate, finding automatically the optimal sink position, and improving the GUI design.

3   GOAT Modules

This subsection introduces only those modules that are later considered in the proposed use-case, i.e., the free-space propagation model, the B-MAC protocol, and the closest-node routing scheme.

3.1   Propagation Models

The physical module implements different radio propagation models in order to determine if a node can be reached from another one, i.e., if a node is in the coverage area of another one. GOAT implements these models to estimate the path loss of a link connecting two nodes, and determine whether they can communicate between each other or not.

Free-Space Path Loss. The free space path-loss model assumes there is only one line-of-sight (LOS) path between the transmitter and the receiver . The power received, P_r, at distance, d, is given by

$$P_r = P_t + G_t + G_r + 20log_{10}\left(\frac{1}{4f\pi d}\right), \tag{1}$$

where P_t is the transmitted signal power, G_t and G_r are the antenna gains of the transmitter and the receiver respectively, and f is the carrier frequency.

3.2   MAC Models

Medium Access Control (MAC) makes possible that several nodes communicate over a shared channel.

B-MAC. B-MAC is a carrier sense MAC for wireless sensor networks that provides a flexible interface with ultra-low power operation, effective collision avoidance, and high channel utilization [1]. B-MAC employs a preamble-sampling scheme to minimize idle listening in order to achieve low power operation. With B-MAC, each sensor node periodically wakes up for few milliseconds (only to check if there is a transmission in the air) and remains awake if it finds activity, otherwise goes again to sleep. A node willing to transmit sends a long preamble before the actual packet transmission. The preamble is large enough to overlap with the listening time of the receiver, thus guaranteeing that the receiver will be awake when the packet is transmitted. The operation of B-MAC is shown in Figure 3, where STA 1 is the transmitting node, STA 2 is the receiving node and STA 3 is experiencing overhearing.

The energy consumed by node i, e_i, in an observation time T_{obs}, can be calculated adding the energy consumed in each of the possible B-MAC node states: transmitting, receiving, overhearing, sampling the channel, and sleeping.

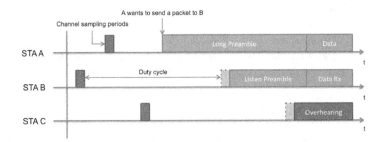

Fig. 3. B-MAC operation

During T_{obs}, the time node i spends in each of the possible states is:

– **Transmitting:** The time node i will spend transmitting during T_{obs} is given by the number of packets it has transmitted (which depends on the node sending rate, λ_t), multiplied by the required time to transmit a single packet, i.e.,

$$T_{tx,i} = \lambda_{t,i} T_{obs} \left(\frac{L_{\text{preamble}} + L_{\text{pkt}}}{R} \right), \tag{2}$$

where L_{preamble} and L_{pkt} are the length of the preamble and the data packet respectively, and R is the transmission rate. Note that $\lambda_{t,i}$ includes both the new packets generated at node i and all packets from other nodes it forwards.

– **Receiving:** The time node i spends receiving packets is given by

$$T_{rx,i} = \lambda_{r,i} T_{obs} \left(\frac{L_{\text{preamble}}}{2R} + \frac{L_{\text{pkt}}}{R} \right), \tag{3}$$

where $\lambda_{r,i}$ is the rate of packets directed to node i. We assume that, on average and because of the preamble-sampling operation, a node will listen half of the transmitted preamble.

– **Overhearing:** The time node i spends receiving packets that are not directed to it is given by

$$T_{ov,i} = \lambda_{o,i} T_{obs} \left(\frac{L_{\text{preamble}}}{2R} + \frac{L_{\text{pkt}}}{R} \right), \tag{4}$$

where $\lambda_{o,i}$ is the rate of packets that node i receives but are not directed to it (i.e., overhearing packets).

– **Sampling the channel:** The time node i spends sampling the channel periodically to detect preambles is given by

$$T_{\text{sp},i} = \frac{T_{\text{sample-dc}}}{T_{\text{sample-dc}} + T_{\text{sleep-dc}}} \left(T_{obs} - (T_{tx,i} + T_{rx,i}) \right), \tag{5}$$

where $T_{\text{sample-dc}}$ is the actual time required to check the channel state and $T_{\text{sleep-dc}}$ is the sleep time in every duty cycle.

– **Sleeping:** The time node i spends in sleeping mode is given by:

$$T_{\text{sl,i}} = \frac{T_{\text{sleep-dc}}}{T_{\text{sample-dc}} + T_{\text{sleep-dc}}} \left(T_{\text{obs}} - (T_{tx,i} + T_{rx,i})\right). \tag{6}$$

It is important to note that $\lambda_{t,i}$, $\lambda_{r,i}$ and $\lambda_{o,i}$ depend on the WSN topology, path-loss and routing models considered. Finding their values for any given topology is one of the most relevant features of GOAT.

Finally, the energy consumed by node i during an observation time is given by

$$e_i = P_{\text{tx}}T_{\text{tx}} + P_{\text{rx}}T_{\text{rx}} + P_{\text{sp}}T_{\text{sp}} + P_{\text{sl}}T_{\text{sl}}. \tag{7}$$

where P_{tx}, P_{rx}, P_{sp} and P_{sl} are the transmitting, receiving, sampling and sleeping power consumption values.

The node i lifetime in time units is given by

$$l_i = \frac{e_{\text{battery}}}{e_i} T_{\text{obs}}, \tag{8}$$

where e_{battery} is the total energy stored in the battery. The total energy stored in the battery is calculated as follows: $3.6 \cdot b_c \cdot V$, where b_c is the battery charge in mAh and V the nominal voltage, which we assume is equal to 1.5 Volts.

3.3   Routing Models

The routing module defines which wireless links will be created in order to allow any sensor node to reach the sink depending on several conditions such as coverage, quality of service (QoS), energy saving, etc.

Closest-Node. Closest-node routing bases the routing on node proximity to the sink. If node i reaches the sink directly, it is linked to the sink. Instead, if node i does not reach the sink, it sweeps all the signals received from the nodes it can reach and determines the level and proximity to each of them. Then, node i will be linked to the node closer to the sink in terms of hops. In case node i reaches two or more nodes placed at the same distance to the sink in number of hops, it will be linked to the closest one of them. That is, node i will be linked to the node from which it receives a higher signal power.

3.4   Configuration Parameters

Some of the variables and parameters defined in GOAT have been hard-coded in the java classes and are not accessible from the GUI. These parameters are not supposed to be modified by the user, as they are part of the different modules. Table 2 lists the hard-coded variables values defined in the first version of GOAT and that are used in the modules presented in this paper.

Table 2. Parameters of the modules used in this paper.

Module		Parameter	Default value
PHY	Hardware	Carrier frequency	2.4 GHz
		Transmission power	1 mW
		Sensitivity	-81 dBm
		Transmission rate	100 kbps
		Transmitting power consumption	60 mW
		Receiving power consumption	40 mW
		Sampling power consumption	10 mW
		Sleeping power consumption	2 mW
	Friis	Transmission gain	0 dBi
		Reception gain	3 dBi
MAC	B-MAC	Data length	100 bytes
		Preamble length	128 bytes
		Checking Time in a Duty Cycle	2 ms
		Sleeping Time in a Duty Cycle	98 ms

4   Use-Case: Plague Tracking

This subsection presents an insect monitoring scenario based on the ENTOMATIC project. ENTOMATIC aims to solve a major problem faced by olive producers: the loss of productivity caused by the olive fruit fly (Bactrocera oleae), with estimated economic losses of approximately 600 euro per hectare.

The solution proposed in the ENTOMATIC project is to develop a WSN formed by autonomous bioacoustics sensors able to detect the olive fly population in the olive orchards. This infrastructure will allow olive producers to track the fly populations in almost real-time and receive advice on when it is necessary the application of pesticides.

ENTOMATIC forecasts the deployment of WSNs with a density of 2-4 bioacoustics sensors per hectare. The lifetime of the networks is expected to be of at least 6 months.

This study aims to analyze the impact of the amount of nodes (and density) on the lifetime of feasible plague tracking WSN scenarios to determine in which cases the minimum network lifetime of 6 months (180 days) is achieved. The effects of the message sending rate and the battery model on the energy consumption will be also estimated.

We will consider three square areas of 25, 49 and 100 hectares with a variable node density and message sending rate. The three considered areas are:

- Small size: The small scenario area will be 500 x 500 m (25 ha). As an example, one small size scenario is shown in Figure 4.
- Medium size: The medium scenario will be 700 x 700 m (49 ha).
- Large size: The large scenario will be 1,000 x 1,000 m (100 ha).

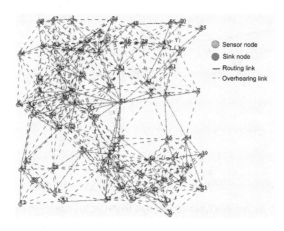

Fig. 4. Small size scenario topology sample

The B-MAC protocol is used in all cases as it has been designed for providing low power operation, effective collision avoidance, and high channel utilization on WSNs with low sending rates; which suits with the proposed plague tracking scenario.

5   Performance Evaluation

In this section, we present the results obtained in the three evaluation tests shown in Table 3. Unless otherwise is stated, in the evaluation presented below we are considering a density of **3 nodes per hectare** and an average message sending rate of **4 packets/hour** per node because they are expected to be the common parameters for ENTOMATIC WSNs. All values presented are the result of averaging three randomly generated network topologies. To compute the network lifetime, we will consider the node that consumes more energy, and therefore has a shorter lifetime.

Table 3. Evaluation Tests

Test	Area	Node density	Sending rate	Physical	Battery
Network Size	**All areas**	Variable	4 packets/h	Free-space	2x AA
Battery Capacity	Small	Variable	4 packets/h	Free-space	**All batteries**
Message Sending rate	**All areas**	3 nodes/ha	Variable	Free-space	2x AA

5.1   Results

Network Size. Figure 5 shows the WSN lifetime when the node density (δ) increases. For low node densities (i.e., 1 node/ha), the lifetime achieved in all three scenarios is very similar, regardless of the area size. Instead, as node density increases, these differences become more pronounced. We can note that in the largest area considered, we will not be able to deploy a WSN with a density of 5 or more nodes per hectare due to its lifetime is lower than 6 months.

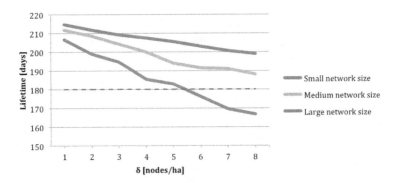

Fig. 5. Network size analysis: lifetime vs. node density

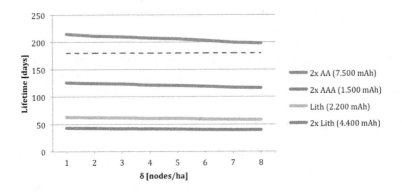

Fig. 6. Battery capacity analysis: lifetime vs. node density

Battery capacity. As shown in (8), the battery level has a linear impact on the lifetime. As expected, Figure 6, is composed of parallel lines that decrease as the node density increases. In this case, the only battery model that reaches the lifetime target is a combination of two AAA batteries.

Message sending rate. Figure 7 shows the WSN lifetime when the packet sending rate (λ) grows. Similarly to the *Network size* test scenario, when λ is small, the lifetime between the three considered area sizes is similar. As the packet sending rate increases, however, the lifetime decreases faster on large areas. For the considered values, the lifetime requirements will be reached for less than 20 pkts/hour in the small area, until 12 pkts/hour in the medium area, and less than 7 pkts/hour in the large area.

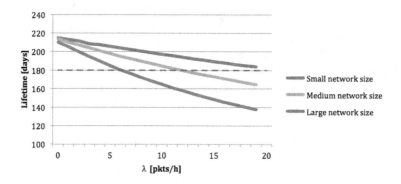

Fig. 7. Message sending rate analysis: lifetime vs. sending rate

5.2   Discussion

From the results presented above, we can conclude that the factor that really impacts on the energy consumption is the number of nodes more than the node density. For instance, comparing the small scenario with 8 nodes/ha (200 nodes), with the large scenario with 2 nodes/ha (200 nodes), we get a similar lifetime in both cases (approximately 198 days). This is because most of the energy consumed at the sensor nodes close to the sink (which are those nodes that usually limit the WSN lifetime) is highly depending on the number of packets they receive, which, in both cases, is similar.

6   Conclusions

This paper presents GOAT, a software tool to plan WSNs. WSNs are one of the top emerging technologies that are changing the way we understand communications, with an expected huge growth rate during the next decades. However, the limited energy resources of sensor nodes are a top constraint in this kind of networks due to the fact that, in most cases, nodes are battery-powered devices and, consequently, energy-constrained. Hence, the main concern is how to reduce the energy consumption in order to extend the overall network lifetime while providing a high enough performance. In order to face that issue, it is almost imperative to test WSN designs and try to optimize the energy saving mechanisms before actually building them. Nonetheless, running real experiments on WSN testbeds is costly and challenging. That is one of the main reasons why we have developed the GOAT tool.

GOAT is a graphical WSN planning tool that allows designing WSNs and estimating its energy consumption in configurable scenarios. The implemented models (physical, battery, MAC, and routing) can be thoroughly set, which offers a vast number of possible scenarios and allows designing and testing future real operating WSNs. As a first version, the tool can be further enhanced in several aspects; nevertheless, we have managed to study a feasible WSN scenario where GOAT has served to estimate the lifetime and energy consumption depending on input variables such as node density or message sending rate.

Moreover, GOAT is intended to be an open project, and due to its software modularity, it is a prototype where new models and protocols can be included and improved. As a modular-based simulator, it is feasible to increase the number of propagation models and MAC and routing protocols.

Acknowledgements. This work has been partially supported by the European Commission through the project FP7-SME-2013-60507-ENTOMATIC, the Spanish Government through the project TEC2012-32354 (Plan Nacional I+D), and by the Catalan Government through the project SGR2009#00617.

References

1. Polastre, J., Hill, J., Culler, D.: Versatile low power media access for wireless sensor networks. In: Proceedings of the 2nd International Conference on Embedded Networked Sensor Systems, pp. 95–107. ACM (2004)
2. Buettner, M., Yee, G.V., Anderson, E., Han, R.: X-mac: a short preamble mac protocol for duty-cycled wireless sensor networks. In: Proceedings of the 4th International Conference on Embedded Networked Sensor Systems, pp. 307–320. ACM (2006)
3. Cano, C., Bellalta, B., Sfairopoulou, A., Barceló, J.: A low power listening mac with scheduled wake up after transmissions for wsns. IEEE Communications Letters **13**(4), 221–223 (2009)
4. Adame, T., Bel, A., Bellalta, B., Barcelo, J., Oliver, M.: IEEE 802.11 ah: the WiFi approach for M2M communications. IEEE Wireless Communications **21**(6), 144–152 (2014)
5. Cano, C., Bellalta, B., Sfairopoulou, A., Oliver, M.: Low energy operation in wsns: A survey of preamble sampling mac protocols. Computer Networks **55**(15), 3351–3363 (2011)
6. Sergio Barrachina. GOAT: Development of a Wireless Sensor Network analysis tool. Technical report (2015)
7. Novel automatic and stand-alone integrated pest management tool for remote count and bioacoustic identification of the Olive Fruit Fly (Bactrocera oleae) in the field. FP7 European Project. (2015) Website: http://entomatic.upf.edu/

Author Index

Printed in the United States
By Bookmasters